Marriage License Fraud

What every Christian couple should know…
before signing a marriage license.

By:
Joshua Paul

Library of Congress Control Number: 2015907428

Marriage License Fraud Publishing House

Huron, South Dakota

MarriageLicenseFraud.com
JesusisLord@marriagelicensefraud.com

Disclaimer: This information is provided and sold with the knowledge that the publisher and author do not offer any legal or other professional advice. In the case of a need for any such expertise consult with an appropriate legal professional. Please see full disclaimer located in the back of the book. Thank you.

Updated 07/23/2022 Chapter 10 Adultery Divorce & Vows

ISBN-13: 978-0692439371

DEDICATION

I dedicate this book to the Lord Jesus Christ. Secondly, I dedicate this book to the individuals seeking truth on the topic of marriage with regards to the legalities surrounding the nature of this relationship.

CONTENTS

"As believers, we are to be seekers of Truth. Not just in the area of our faith but in all areas and aspects of our lives, Truth is Truth. Joshua Paul brings a very biblical and very important message on how, "God's people perish for a lack of knowledge." The enemy will do his very best to deceive God's people into opening doors that will allow him to steal, kill and destroy. He has been doing so from the beginning. Joshua Paul exposes what most would look at as a very positive thing, the marriage license is actually a contract with far more reaching implications than we could imagine. Marriage License Fraud is a must read for anyone who is married or looking to get married. This is actually one of, if not the biggest puzzle piece as to why marriages are failing in this nation. The state marriage license is a spiritual problem at the root and if it is not dealt with, things will only get worse." – C. Toda

"Joshua has written a challenging book for all married Christians and those considering marriage. Those who desire to honor G-d in their marriage would be wise to get this book." – D. Spitz

"Wow Wow Wow Wow!!!!

I was absolutely ASTONISHED at how well researched it was. It took me a while to read as my husband wanted to read it WITH me. Too many books identify a problem and do not offer solutions. The entire book was so incredible. I must admit that the bible is the only book that I have ever highlighted and I have to say that in this book, I highlighted so many awesome points that I had to eventually quit because half of every page was bright yellow!! I resorted to paragraph brackets. Lol! Seriously, it has changed my husbands view and reassured him on our right and spirit led decision.

We both learned so much and are so grateful for the book.

What a timely message!!! Definitely recommending it to all of my friends!" - L. Sipe

ACKNOWLEDGMENTS

Thank you to my friends and family who encouraged me in this project. Thank you to all the people who read, gave feedback and edited this book. Thank you to all the people who shared their experiences, wisdom and insight on the intricacies of marriage.

I have learned from each of you and am grateful.

1

ORIGIN AND HISTORY OF MARRIAGE LICENSES

What is the Origin of State Licensing?

The origin of "State Licensing" began primarily within the Roman Catholic system. In the 1500's the Roman Catholics controlled much of life surrounding the rules and regulations of how the family unit conducted itself. Going as far back as the Council of Trent, "decrees" were passed by the Roman Catholic church as legislature to hedge in the Protestant movement and reform the Roman Catholic system. It was in this time period, that the Council of Trent determined marriage to be conducted before the parish priest or with a license by a "non-ordained Roman Catholic priest," in the presence of witnesses.

The purpose of this legislature was to force Baptists, Protestants and others to stop marrying in their own churches. Roman Catholics worked to prevent the

Protestant movement from performing their own ceremonies. Protestants had an increasing desire to separate themselves from these civil authorities and ultimately the Pope. The Pope is seen as the spiritual leader who determines the laws and regulations for all Catholics, rather than Jesus.

Eventually groups within the Protestant reformation rejected the idea of being subject to the dictates of the Roman Catholic system and civil authorities. Couples began coming together in holy matrimony within the congregations they fellowshipped. Christians who married within their congregations were falsely accused of advocating immorality and depravity.

One such couple who married outside the Roman Catholic system were imprisoned. In 1551, Jeronimus Segerson wrote a letter to his wife Lyksen, "Grace, peace, gladness, joy and comfort, a firm faith, good confidence, with ardent love to God, I wish my most beloved wife, Lyksen Dirks, whom I married in the presence of God and his holy church, and too thus agreeably to the Lord's command to be my wife."

She replied with the following, "My dear husband in the Lord, whom I married before God and His people, but with whom they say I have lived in adultery, because I was not married in Baal: the Lord saith, 'rejoice when men shall say all manner of evil against you; rejoice and be exceedingly glad, for great is your reward in heaven."

This couple understood the ramifications of the marriage license. The license would bind them, to Catholic civil authority. The outcome of this contract would make the individual subservient to whichever department or agency is tied to the license. The licensee submits to the regulations the agency had placed in the contract[1].

The first marriage between Adam and Eve was initiated, by God. All throughout the Bible we see permission extended to the patriarch of the family or parents.

Protestants Move Away from Catholics

Why were the Protestants and Baptists so eager to get away from the Roman Catholic system or specifically their doctrine? "Aren't they all "Christian?" A common misconception regarding Roman Catholic doctrine and religious system, needs to be addressed.

No doubt there are those in Catholic parishes who have relationship with Jesus and look only to Him for their salvation alone. However, the Roman Catholic "doctrine" (what is taught - Catechism) regarding how one must be saved and enter eternal life, communicates a false sense of salvation because it is not actual Bible Scripture. Catechism doctrine declares, "…Catechism expounds revelation..." another quote would include, "The plan of this catechism is inspired by the great tradition of catechism which build catechesis on four pillars: the baptismal profession of faith

[1]http://www.drbentownsend.com/documents/the%20marriage%20license.pdf

(the Creed), the sacraments of faith, the life of faith (the Commandments), and the prayer of the believer (the Lord's Prayer)." Basically, Catechism could be seen as a commentary, expounding revelation and Catholic tradition. Does every parish teach out of the Roman Catholic Catechism, God only knows? Visiting every parish is an impossibility. It is my hope that some of these parishes would have born-again believers, teaching Hebrew Scriptures and the New Testament Covenant from the Bible, not Catholic tradition in the form of Catechism.

Here is a list of some of the false doctrinal teachings:

- Purgatory is not in the Bible and does not exist
- Infant baptism does not ensure salvation - See Acts 8:36-37
- Praying to "virgin Mary" or the saints is idolatry – See John 14:13
- Works based salvation (penance & indulgence) – See Romans 10:9
- Pope-Pontiff – is not the bridge maker to God – See Acts 4:10-12

Protestants desired to disconnect from the Roman Catholic system for varying reasons, some of those reasons are mentioned above. The false teachings and over reaching control placed upon the people by the Roman Catholics, led to this divide.

Here are some links discussing Catholic teachings further:

https://carm.org/list-of-roman-catholic-false-teachings

http://www.vatican.va/archive/ENG0015/__P5.HTM

http://www.vatican.va/archive/ENG0015/_INDEX.HTM

The History of Marriage License in the USA

The founding fathers of the United States, did not want a state-church similar to England or a church-state similar to France and Spain. William Blackstone advised against civil law ideas. He stated, "The civil law was partly of pagan origin." Common law marriage originated from England in the middle ages and was also adopted in this nation after the Revolutionary war. State licensing began when blacks and whites married because at the time, this was an illegal act or relationship. So licensing this type of relationship was the only alternative the government had. Eventually, the States had a meeting to abolish common law marriage all together and put marriage under statutory (civil) law (why did this come about. The reader would want to know what changed that would cause the states to abolish common law marriage). The two outcomes the state license achieves are revenue streams and it creates a system of control. The result of this decision once again placed married couples under civil authorities, rather than under church authority. This was an entirely legal move to put the church under the authority of the state and civil authorities because participation was "voluntary." Any time the minister in a marriage ceremony closes by stating, "By the power or authority vested in by the state of ...." the minister is now under the governor of the state's authority. There is no difference between the minister or a judicial representative of the state.

The mixture of civil law and God's law in the arena of marriage causes a problem because marriage is a God given right for a man and woman to marry each other. The state can only go so far as to simply make this issue entirely "directory" or another way of saying it, “voluntary.”

The history of the marriage license was developed in the southern parts of the United States of America where blacks and whites were beginning to "intermarry." North Carolina and Tennessee were two of the first states to issue a "marriage license." In the 1800’s it was illegal for blacks and whites to marry. Miscegenation law is another legal term used by the government to prevent inter-racial marriage.

In the mid 1800's there were approximately half a million "free negroes" in the USA. At the time, the culturally or social accepted norms were of the thought "negroes" were inferior to "whites." The attitude of the day was, “If you are black, you must be a slave." Therefore while the Emancipation Proclamation had taken place the "negroes" were free only in name. The prevailing attitude of the day continued to legislate civil law year after year requiring "licenses" for just about anything and everything, including but not limited to: carrying papers to prove freedom, gun permits, occupational and business licensing, church congregation supervision of a licensed white minister, permits to travel freely, etc. What can be gleaned from this example? The business of licensing is used to control a group of people through the regulations of the state. Complete freedom is not possible in such an environment.

Up until this time, people were generally entering into marriage under "common law" or through unlicensed religious marriages. Marriage, for the believer is a relational status between husband, and wife, with a commitment before God .

Only a very small percent of society was participating in miscegenation, an act that was considered illegal. Take a look at what happened in 1911 which ultimately led to the marriage license reality we see today.

American Uniform Marriage & Marriage License Act

In 1909, several states gathered together on the topic of marriage. The purpose behind the gathering was two fold. The first objective was to abolish the idea of common law marriage. The second objective was to make the license an absolute pre-requisite to marriage. As you will read below their intentions were clearly communicated. This meeting was titled:

American Uniform Marriage & Marriage License Act

AN ACT

"The following Act "Relating to and Regulating Marriage and Marriage Licenses" was first considered by the National Conference of Commissioners on Uniform State Laws at Detroit in August, 1909.

At that meeting the Committee on Marriage and Divorce was directed so to shape the Act **that** *"Common Law*

Marriages" should be abolished. This was effected by making the issuance of a license to marry an absolute prerequisite (subject to one saving clause, see Section XXIV), and by requiring that the marriage be properly solemnized. At the meeting of the Conference in Chattanooga in August, 1910, the Act was more or less amended, and was referred back to the Committee to incorporate the amendments and such other desired changes as they should deem advisable. At Boston in August, 1911, the Act in its present form was finally adopted, and ordered to be printed and circulated by November, 1911, for submissions to the Legislatures of the several States[2].

Walter George SmithPresident of the Conference

Philadelphia, PA.November 1, 1911"

The entire marriage license act was adopted by all 50 states in 1929. Hollywood helped propagandize the state license program in movies such as the 1934 Academy Award winning film, "It Happened One Night." The closing comments in this film ends with dialogue of a married couple referring to the two stars in the movie, "I do not even think they're married?! Yes, they are. I saw the marriage license."

Miscegenation Laws Made Illegal

Blacks Law defines **Miscegenation**[3] as, sexual relations

[2] American Uniform Marriage and Marriage License Act

[2] Miscegenation - by permission Blacks Law Dictionary 10th edition

between races; esp., the production of offspring by parents of different races, usu. when and where considered illegal. In 1967, the U.S. Supreme Court held that laws banning interracial marriages are unconstitutional because of Loving vs. Virginia[4].

Uniform Marriage & Divorce Act

Eventually "The Uniform Marriage and Divorce Act" (UMDA) was established in 1970, which allowed for marriage dissolution or divorce for any reason. One individual can divorce the other without finding fault whatsoever. Prior to this act people needed to prove fault of the other party such as desertion, adultery, alcoholism, physical abuse, etc. In Part III of the UMDA the party leaving the marriage can also collect spousal support from the other party.

The state while it is not suppose to be a business, very much runs as a business (that never becomes profitable). The license serves as the "product" the state is selling to citizens. Every good business wants to find ways to increase revenues. State governments have a vested interest in controlling moral activities by licensing those activities, thereby, generating income. Taxation on liquor, tobacco, gambling, prostitution are examples of activities requiring a state license.

[4] https://www.law.cornell.edu/supremecourt/text/388/1

We see the development of the marriage license as a means of generating substantial income for the state. Not only does the state stand to make money when the couple desires to marry by issuing the marriage license, if a couple desires to divorce, they must go to court to seek dissolution of the marriage and pay court fees, attorney fees, filing fees, etc. Each time a couple is married and divorced, the state receives more income. From a revenue standpoint, it is in the state's best interest to see marriages fail[5]

---

[5] http://www.drbentownsend.com/documents/the%20marriage%20license.pdf

2

Parens Patriae

Parens Patriae is a term that is not too common in our culture today. However, this idea has existed for hundreds of years. This gives a history of how the state sees itself as our parent and/or our child's parent. Our individual relational status depends entirely on how we view ourselves and the agreements we sign off on.

Blacks Law Defines:

Parens Patriae[6]: [Latin "parent of his or her country"]

1. The state regarded as sovereign' the state in its capacity as provider of protection to those unable to care for themselves.

[6] By permission Blacks Law Dictionary 10th edition Dictionary

2. A doctrine by which a government has standing to prosecute a lawsuit on behalf of a citizen, esp. on behalf of someone who is under legal disability to prosecute the suit <parens patriae allowed the state to institute proceedings>

The state ordinarily has no standing to sue on behalf of its citizens, unless a separate, sovereign interest will be served by the suit.

"The *parens patriae* doctrine has its roots in English Common Law. In feudal times various obligations and powers, collectively referred to as the "royal prerogative," were reserved to the king. The king exercised these functions in *his role of father of the country.*

In the United States, the *parens patriae* doctrine has had its greatest application in the *treatment of children, mentally ill persons, and other individuals who are legally incompetent to manage their affairs.* The state is the supreme guardian of all children within its jurisdiction, and state courts have the inherent power to intervene to protect the best interests of children whose welfare is jeopardized by controversies between parents. This inherent power is generally supplemented by legislative acts that define the scope of child protection in a state.

The state, acting as *parens patriae*, can make decisions regarding mental health treatment on behalf of one who is mentally incompetent to make the decision on his or her own behalf, but the extent of the state's intrusion is limited to reasonable and necessary treatment.

The doctrine of *parens patriae* has been expanded in the United States to permit the attorney general of a state to commence litigation for the benefit of state residents for federal antitrust violations (15 U.S.C.A. § 15c). This authority is intended to further the public trust, safeguard the general and economic welfare of a state's residents, protect residents from illegal practices, and assure that the benefits of federal law are not denied to the general population.

States may also invoke *parens patriae* to protect interests such as the health, comfort, and welfare of the people, interstate water rights, and the general economy of the state. For a state to have standing to sue under the doctrine, it must be more than a nominal party without a real interest of its own and must articulate an interest apart from the interests of particular private parties.[7]"

The state, through licensing is letting people "voluntarily" self- identify with one of the three categories:

1. Child

[7] Reference: TheFreeDictionary © 2015 by Farlex, Inc. http://legal-dictionary.thefreedictionary.com/Parens+Patriae

2. Mentally ill person
3. Legally incompetent to manage their affairs

Whichever one a person chooses, it does not matter. Therefore, they will "manage" whomever's marital relationship and affairs as occasion arises. The state will gladly tell people what to do, when to do it, and how to do it, if allowed. Married couples who sign the marriage license are in fact giving control to the state, as if they are children, mentally ill or too incompetent to manage themselves, their marriage and their family.

Braveheart

Braveheart conveys a great example of *parens patriae.* This movie demonstrates the attitude and perspective of the state government towards the people. Using the marriage license, people are in affect handing-over their rights to the state. The state becomes parent to their children and sovereign over the marriage relationship.

In the beginning of the movie, Braveheart, King Edward Longshanks makes the quote, "The trouble with Scotland is that it is full of Scot's. Perhaps the time has come to re-institute an old custom. Perhaps then Prima nocte? First night, when any common girl inhabiting their lands is married, our nobles shall have sexual rights to her on the night of her wedding. If we cannot get them out, we will breed them out. That should fetch just the kind of lord's we want in Scotland. Taxes or no taxes, huh?"

In the following scene, a nobleman intrudes on a Scottish wedding, by announcing, "I've come to claim the right of Prima nocte. As lord of these lands I will bless this marriage by taking the Bride into my bed on the first night of her union. It is my noble right." The English nobleman claims "his right" to what in the movie is called "Prima Nocte or Noctis." This law allows the English nobles to have sexual relations with the Scottish peasant virgins on their wedding night. The implications of this will lead to the first born of all Scottish families will be of English and Scottish heritage. A bastardized nation will ensue. English and Scottish breeding cause the first born to be left without it's true father, divested loyalties and identity.

Prima nocte was a way for "government" to control marriages, families and economies. This is very much what the state is doing with the marriage license, attaching itself to holy matrimony.

Parens patriae or prima nocte (as it is called in Braveheart) has taken place throughout history. Such ideology is one of control.

Notice, they do not simply establish a law allowing a nobleman to sleep with the peasant girl, upon becoming an adult. Why do they specifically force this issue on the night of the wedding ceremony? It is for the purpose of taking control over the family unit and marriages, while maintaining a taxable enterprise. In the past, if a man was not committed to a woman or the family, both woman and baby would have less chance of survival. The ruling system cannot afford to have all the unwed women bearing children without support. The whole purpose is to maintain a system of control, so the ruling class could still tax the peasants. The nobles needed a population for support, so they themselves actually did not have to work.

The entire story line of Braveheart is a depiction of what is transpiring in our society. Currently, the government in the USA is growing like a monster, requiring more money from the population in order to maintain control over the population. We currently experience increased taxes and more governmental jobs that do not drive an economy, but help maintain control. We see elected officials who receive high salaries and campaign and lobbyist funding. The game that was played so many years ago with the nobles and peasants, still plays out today through our political system.

In Braveheart, the Scottish "nobles" (who were under the rule of the English nobles but above the peasant class - middle class for lack of a better description) never wanted to fight for their freedom because they could politically negotiate for more lands and titles. In essence they were being bribed or bought off. They were happy as long as they were taken care of and not living the peasant life. The Scottish nobles had no loyalty to the common man. Loyalty only remained to their purses. William makes a speech to Scottish nobles and says to them, "You're so concerned with squabbling for the scraps from Longshanks table that you have missed your God given right for something better. There is a difference between us. You think the people of this country exist to provide you with position. I think your position exists to provide those people with freedom and I am going to see that they have it!"

Robert the Bruce, the King in waiting, to Scotland, follows William out the door "Wait. I respect what you said. But remember that these men have lands and cattle, much to risk." William follows up with, "And the common man that bleeds on the battle field does he risk less?"

A righteous government is designed to serve the needs of the people in such a way so they are free to live a life of prosperity, not oppression. When an unrighteous government is in power the people are oppressed with taxes and unjust laws. We are seeing this take place more and more in this country. Currently, taxes are increasing and the civil statutes are being corrupted because of the love of money. Laws are established because special interest groups are buying politicians. Laws condoning baby killing (abortion) and sexual perversion are being accepted in various forms. Our fiat monetary system is totally corrupted. This nation is anything but free. There may not be chains and shackles hanging on our wrists and feet, but I assure you they are there through the agreements we make. The shackles just look a little different in this digital age. The founding fathers and the men who fought for freedom in years gone by would be dismayed to see the current state of affairs regarding this nation.

King Longshanks after learning William invaded the city of York says, "I will offer a truce and buy him off." This is the state mentality. The state gives as little as it can to maintain a perception of power and control. Rather than do what is right for all the people, Longshanks is willing to give a little to one man, Wallace, who leads the destiny of Scotland.

Somehow, the government in America, has convinced the people of the supposed benefits of signing up for the state marriage license. There are no additional benefits for married couples who have signed a state Marriage License versus those who have not. We are defrauded by the state into thinking there are additional benefits, when there are none.

In the next scene, the Princess of England, was sent on behalf of King Longshanks to offer the bribe to William Wallace. She says to William, "The King desires peace. He proposes you withdraw your attack. In return, he grants you title, states and this chest of gold."

William replies, "Lordship and titles, gold! That I should become Judas?!"

The Princess replies, "Peace is made in such ways."

To which William quickly follows up, "Slaves are made in

such ways!!!

A Society of Virtue?

The sad reality of the world today is people are so easily bought off with bribes or willing to settle for much less. Ideals, integrity and justice have been so perverted by men and women who compromise for the sake of money, looking out for their own interests. Politicians have tough jobs. Sadly, it seems so many have sold out the American people to fatten their own wallets. Can we start to look out for the interests of others for the good of all? We must become a people of "virtue" again. It is disappointing to see how people have, walked away from virtue and handed their freedoms over to the controlling ruling class.

Virtue: morally good behavior or character: a good and moral quality: the good result that comes from something[8].

God intended marriage to be a holy and sacred union. The enemy wants to do everything he can to throw a wrench into what God desires. The wedding day is the foundational point of the new life created between husband, wife and children to follow. This will be explored further in the next chapter.

---

[8] Virtue - By permission. From Merriam-Webster's Collegiate® Dictionary, 11th Edition ©2015 by Merriam-Webster, Inc. (www.Merriam-Webster.com).

3

IS THE GOVERNMENT HOLY?

Are any of the governmental agencies, holy, according to the Word of God?

Let's start by defining some terms here so we all know exactly what we are talking about.

Holy[9]: exalted or worthy of complete devotion as one perfect in goodness and righteousness; divine ...

Divine[10]: of, relating to, or proceeding directly from God or a god; being a deity; directed to a deity; supremely good.

---

[9] [9] Holy - By permission. From Merriam-Webster's Collegiate® Dictionary, 11th Edition ©2015 by Merriam-Webster, Inc. (www.Merriam-Webster.com

[10] [10] Divine By permission. From Merriam-Webster's Collegiate® Dictionary, 11th Edition ©2015 by Merriam-Webster, Inc. (www.Merriam-Webster.com

Let us look up deity as it is not common everyday language.

Deity[11]**:** the rank or essential nature of a god; a god or goddess; one exalted or revered as supremely good or powerful

The Interlinear Bible defines Holy as well:

Holy: apartness, sacredness, holiness

And you shall be to Me a kingdom of priests and a holy nation.' These [are] the words which you shall speak to the children of Israel." – (Exodus 19:6 NKJV)

but as He who called you [is] holy, you also be holy in all [your] conduct, because it is written, "Be holy, for I am holy." – (1 Peter 1:15-16 NKJV)

---

[11] Deity - By permission. From Merriam-Webster's Collegiate® Dictionary, 11th Edition ©2015 by Merriam-Webster, Inc. (www.Merriam-Webster.com

But you [are] a chosen generation, a royal priesthood, a holy nation, His own special people, that you may proclaim the praises of Him who called you out of darkness into His marvelous light; - (1 Peter 2:9 NKJV)

For we do not wrestle against flesh and blood, but against principalities, against powers, against the rulers of the darkness of this age, against spiritual [hosts] of wickedness in the heavenly [places]. (Ephesians 6:12 NKJV)

There are technically only two governments at work in the earth, the Kingdom of Heaven and the kingdom of darkness. The principalities, powers and the rulers of darkness largely run the Federal and state governments. The world government system is moving forward by the hand of the evil one, increasingly day by day. The good news is the Kingdom of God is advancing more deeply and powerfully than the world system ever could. Amen.

11 "Now I am no longer in the world, but these are in the world, and I come to You. Holy Father, keep through Your name those whom You have given Me, that they may be one as We [are].

12 "While I was with them in the world, I kept them in Your name. Those whom You gave Me I have kept; and none of them is lost except the son of perdition, that the Scripture might be fulfilled.

13 "But now I come to You, and these things I speak in the world, that they may have My joy fulfilled in themselves.

14 "I have given them Your word; and the world has hated them because they are not of the world, just as I am not of the world.

15 "I do not pray that You should take them out of the world, but that You should keep them from the evil one.

16 "They are not of the world, just as I am not of the world.

17 "Sanctify them by Your truth. Your word is truth.

18 "As You sent Me into the world, I also have sent them into the world.

19 "And for their sakes I sanctify Myself, that they also may be sanctified by the truth. (John 17:11-19 NKJV)

Are there righteous men and women in our government? Yes. There are a few that have found the narrow path and are called to be in the world government system to influence for the Kingdom of

God. The Most High uses each of us in unique and wonderful ways. For this discussion look at the overall picture of what is currently taking place.

Covenant Agreement

Whether we know it or not, couples are yoking themselves with an institution and body of law that is condoning "child sacrifice or "abortion," murder, stealing, fornication, adultery and a laundry list of other sins. We are putting marriages under a body of laws that go directly against the Word of God.

We have mentioned covenant in the previous chapter, let's define it according to Black's Law Dictionary. now.

Covenant[12]: A formal agreement or promise, usu. in a contract.

It seems as though this marriage license agreement would fall under that of a "contract" or "covenant." Consider God's warnings and promises in Deuteronomy 7 for His people.

A Closer Look at Deuteronomy 7:1-16

[12] Covenant - Permission by Black's Law Dictionary, 10th ed. 2014

"When the LORD your God brings you into the land which you go to possess, and has cast out many nations before you, the Hittites and the Girgashites and the Amorites and the Canaanites and the Perizzites and the Hivites and the Jebusites, seven nations greater and mightier than you,

Each of these nations including Egypt have their own set of laws, rules and regulations that God said were ungodly, evil and wicked. God gave His people a different way of life. He gave them His own laws, statutes and judgments of righteousness.

"and when the LORD your God delivers them over to you, you shall conquer them [and] utterly destroy them. You shall make no covenant with them nor show mercy to them.

Notice how he states, "make no covenant (contract)" with them. Why do you think that is? Let us keep reading His Word for the answers.

"Nor shall you make marriages with them. You shall not give your daughter to their son, nor take their daughter for your son.

Interesting to point this out in verse 2 - make no

covenant - verse 3 - nor shall you make marriages with them. Later we will see how, the state of Ohio plainly communicates in their statutes, by signing a marriage licenses we are completely disobeying Deuteronomy 7:2-3. We are "covenanting" or "contracting" with other nations or other body of law outside the Word of God and "marrying with them." The Ohio marriage license clearly states that it is a three way contract.

"For they will turn your sons away from following Me, to serve other gods; so the anger of the LORD will be aroused against you and destroy you suddenly.

Is not this happening in the USA? Aren't children rebelling against their biological parents, following the way of the state or world and turning their hearts away from the Living God? Again the United States of America as a collective body of people entertains and part-takes with the sins of adultery, fornication, homosexuality, perversion of all kinds, pornography, molestation, rape, divorce and children being conceived out of wedlock (some of them being murdered in the womb), it seems that one might make a case verse 4 is coming to pass.

It is virtually impossible to tangibly quantify the impact our actions have in the spirit realm. We do know the spirit realm is more real than the things that are seen, as stated in Hebrews 11:3. No doubt, the principalities and powers are able to use our agreements to gain entry points into our lives, without our knowledge of this taking place.

But thus you shall deal with them: you shall destroy their altars, and break down their [sacred] pillars, and cut down their wooden images, and burn their carved images with fire.

"For you [are] a holy people to the LORD your God; the LORD your God has chosen you to be a people for Himself, a special treasure above all the peoples on the face of the earth.

What a great verse! We are to be "holy" or "separate" to the LORD. He has chosen us for Himself, not to be shared with the other "nations." What a beautiful picture. God is jealous for us and does not want to share me with any other god, lover or nation. Let us be jealous for Him, not willing to share our affections, agreements with any entity apart from Him.

This Scripture comes to mind of Jesus' words:

14 "I have given them Your word; and the world has hated them
because they are not of the world, just as I am not of the world. 15
"I do not pray that You should take them out of the world, but

that You should keep them from the evil one. 16 "They are not of the world, just as I am not of the world. 17 "Sanctify them by Your truth. Your word is truth. (John 17:14-17 NKJV)

This verse might be stated another way, in the world but not yoked to it because we want to take Jesus' yoke… which is easy and connected to Him, not to the world. Covenants are contracts, contracts are agreements and agreements are attachments, which seems like we should not want to attach to this world system in any capacity as much as possible.

"The LORD did not set His love on you nor choose you because you were more in number than any other people, for you were the least of all peoples;

"but because the LORD loves you, and because He would keep the oath which He swore to your fathers, the LORD has brought you out with a mighty hand, and redeemed you from the house of bondage, from the hand of Pharaoh king of Egypt.

He is faithful to keep His oath, covenant or contract. He has pulled us out of the house of bondage. The state has become a house of bondage and a form of Egypt or Babylon.

"Therefore know that the LORD your God, He [is] God, the

faithful God who keeps covenant and mercy for a thousand generations with those who love Him and keep His commandments;

God is faithful to keep His covenant. He is unchanging and faithful for a thousand generations! He is so good! Do you think the government is faithful and merciful like YHWH (Yahweh – God)? Let us choose covenant with Him. He alone is trustworthy.

"and He repays those who hate Him to their face, to destroy them. He will not be slack with him who hates Him; He will repay him to his face.

"Therefore you shall keep the commandment, the statutes, and the judgments which I command you today, to observe them.

"Then it shall come to pass, because you listen to these judgments, and keep and do them, that the LORD your God will keep with you the covenant and the mercy which He swore to your fathers.

"And He will love you and bless you and multiply you; He will also bless the fruit of your womb and the fruit of your land, your grain and your new wine and your oil, the increase of your cattle and the offspring of your flock, in the land of which He swore to your fathers to give you.

Verse 13 has amazing promises for the family. Look at what He promises when we choose to covenant with Him. He will bring forth increase upon our lives." *You shall be blessed above all peoples ; there shall not be a male or female barren among you or among your livestock.*

"And the LORD will take away from you all sickness, and will afflict you with none of the terrible diseases of Egypt which you have known, but will lay [them] on all those who hate you.

"Also you shall destroy all the peoples whom the LORD your God delivers over to you; your eye shall have no pity on them; nor shall you serve their gods, for that [will be] a snare to you. (Deuteronomy 7:1-16 NKJV)

Such beautiful promises to God's people for following His Way. If we follow His Way, we do not need another option or solution provided by the state. We will be holy unto Him. Atheists, Agnostics, Unbelievers may need or desire the state's laws, statutes and judgments. God's people simply need His Word, obedience and love – we only need His way. As the book of James 1:25 describes God's law, "the perfect law of liberty." He wants to make covenant with us. He wants to protect us. He wants us to set our affections on Him alone. He wants to keep us from defilement.

Again, there is no communication piece about a state marriage license covenant in the Bible. Just because something is not discussed or mentioned, does not mean there is no context for it in society today. We drive automobiles and there is no mention of them in the Bible. I get that argument. Some people out there agree, that we should not have driver's licenses either. Such battles can be left for another conversation. The question is, what gives the state the right to license something as holy and of God as marriage? Only God creates and establishes two people in a marriage, not the state.

Remember, Jesus fulfilled the law on the cross at Calvary. I am not advocating looking to the law for salvation of sins, but as a way of living, so as to prevent one's self from becoming defiled by the world. Perhaps God's people have made agreements that have tied God's hands, in a sense? Therefore preventing the fullness of His blessings to flow unhindered? People make inner vows that require undoing regularly. It makes sense that outward vows would also need to be undone. In this case, the state marriage license would be a prime example.

Conception from Heaven's Perspective

I was at a friend's house and he shared a vision he had regarding the conception of a baby in Heaven. He was kind enough to share what he saw:

CONCEPTION OF A CHILD

ALL HEAVEN CELEBRATES THE MOMENT

"Jesus showed me the scene and said "All heaven celebrates at the moment a child is conceived. During the celebration the angel Michael stands up, then trumpets are blown drawing attention to Michael shouting out the proclamation of the destiny of who that child is meant to be, calling them by name. Because Satan and his demons were in heaven at creation, they have the right and ability to hear these proclamations, giving them insight from conception, on how to possibly sidetrack their destiny. It is very important for fathers to pray into the destiny of their children from the moment of conception, forward. This is one of the most important responsibilities and privileges of being a father. You get to, and must help shape and form their destinies".

All things got silent and very serious when Michael stood up and the trumpets blew. It was an indication of how serious this matter is to God. I actually got to watch the celebration and proclamation of one child. People were jumping, shouting, and clapping. It went on for a while, like a group of cheerleaders, calling out the destiny that had just been proclaimed. I was amazed at how big Michael was compared to all others. He was over twenty feet tall!

I also saw heaven groan over the loss of the destiny of a child aborted."

By T. Leverett March 22, 2010

Conception of Marriage

The wedding is the "conception" day of a marriage and family. The conception of a marriage must have a destiny as well. Would not heaven respond in like manner as a baby being conceived? Isn't the same concept taking place? A marriage is being conceived on the wedding day. God has a destiny for every marriage as well because the two individuals have a destiny. Therefore we can conclude the two as one, have a destiny together written in heaven.

For those of you wanting to know where this might be revealed in Scripture, check out Psalm 37, 139 and Jeremiah 29:11 to name a few.

Two people coming together in the sight of God are the first steps to establishing holy offspring and more reward for Jesus Christ because of redeeming mankind. In like manner, would not Satan want to wreck the destiny of a marriage? Would he not fight tooth and nail to ensure all marriages end in destruction? The oneness of marriage is a reflection of the trinity of God. There is no division, no separation, and perfect unity for the Most High. The family unit also is made in the image of God; male, female and children. I am not calling God a female, but focusing on the reality man, woman and child are all created in the image of the Living God, forming a whole unit. The intent of the family is perfect unity, glorifying Jesus.

The State's Righteousness Affects My Marriage?

Here is an analogy of how all marriages and in particular, Christian marriages are affected by the "voluntary" state marriage license. Imagine a Mom who has conceived and become pregnant. The Mom in this story represents the state. The umbilical cord represents the state marriage license. The baby represents the husband and wife marriage relationship. The state controls the marriage, through the connection of the license. Whatever the state feeds on in terms of righteous or unrighteous law, will directly pass through the umbilical cord to the baby. The state decides what to consume and the husband and wife have no voice. Here are two examples:

- Imagine if the Mom eats healthy, organic nutritious food, takes vitamins and minerals, predominantly drinks water, does not drink alcohol, smoke marijuana, cigarettes or do drugs. The Mom lives a healthy life overall. The baby receives healthy food, nutrients, enzymes, and everything necessary to grow strong and healthy because of the umbilical cord.

- Now what if rather than eating well, the Mom only eats fast-food, is an alcoholic, smokes cigarettes, does drugs and participates in other harmful activities. Engaging in these harmful activities will likely affect the long-term health of the baby and possibly compromise the birth.

Practically everything that supports the baby's life is in control and dictated by what the Mom eats, breathes and drinks. Life or death is made in the decisions of the Mom, practically speaking, because she alone chooses. Notice the tremendous responsibility the Mom has for her baby's well being. Our decisions have consequence.

Fifty or sixty years ago the state government was operating in significantly greater alignment with godly principles and perspective, than it is today. Right now the Federal & state government is ever so quickly diving head first into unrighteousness and disagreement with the Word of God. The government is disappointedly, losing sight of any moral compass.

The state and federal government are increasingly being swayed by the popular opinions of the minority. On several occasions, the government has not upheld the people's vote surrounding the topic of marriage. Rather the vote was overturned because of the popular opinion of the minority. The idea of government redefining the definition of marriage is flat out awful. How much pride does one need to have, to think they can come along and redefine a word that has existed since the beginning of time? This shift towards exalting wickedness is reeking havoc on the family unit across the nation. The state marriage license covenant is the umbilical cord to feed the husband and wife nutrients or sludge. The demonic realm gains access to the marriage and family through the covenant agreement the marriage license represents. The more evil the state or federal government become, the more it will be unnecessarily challenging for the marriage to remain intact. Face it, marriage is challenging enough on its own. God's people do not need to be yoked to an unholy, ungodly body of law.

It seems fairly clear that Satan and the principalities and powers of darkness have set up a system to influence the marriage relationship through a legal access point. With the marriage license signed at the "conception" of the marriage, Satan and his minions can access the marriage consistently. Depending on the individuals in a specific marriage, there might be multiple access points – this being a significant one to any marriage. Of course he waits for the absolute weakest point or moment to attack. The goal is to come to that place where like Jesus, we could say, "Satan has nothing in me."

Life is difficult as it is for a baby to grow, become a healthy adult and live to be 100 years old. There are natural troubles and challenges that pop up, without needing any additional help. In today's moral decline the marriage license actually creates an unnecessarily harmful environment for a marriage to properly sustain life. The second example of a Mom feeding on unhealthy poisonous toxins, is what we are seeing from the government system today. In this analogy, the state seems to increasingly feed on more and more wickedness. Obviously this reality is damaging and harmful to the success of the health and life of a full marriage.

Satan on the Ground Floor

If Satan can get in on the ground floor, (i.e. the marriage license), the married couple has no basis for knowing any other reality. There is no other reality the married couple can compare to because it has always been this way. If everyone follows the same protocol then nobody can see a difference in relationship or question the status quo. Putting everyone in the same boat is the governments goal. The old saying is true, "Do not rock the boat." God's people in particular, would be well served to not yoke itself to the unholy state and ungodly body of laws. People are beginning to see the truth, stand for freedom and the freedom of their children. The legal system right now is not a picture of freedom, it's modern day slavery. Our forefathers would be shocked as to what this nation has bowed down to and allowed to transpire.

The work of Satan entirely exists in the playground of ignorance. If people continue to go along with the status quo and do not stop to think or question what is actually transpiring, then he wins.

Paraphrasing Jesus, He says, "... ask, seek, knock. You have not because you ask not." The last thing Satan wants any of us to do is ask questions. Jesus, I ask that You make Your people great "askers."

4

PERMISSION FROM THE STATE

Why are those who call themselves "The Bride of Christ" and "followers of Jesus" going to the state for permission to marry? The reality is, most if not all of us do not really understand what we are doing when we sign the marriage license. Generally, we are simply excited to start a new chapter in life and get married. I certainly did not have any idea the ramifications of the marriage license, until I began asking questions and investigating the matter. Rarely if does anyone ever teach or communicate to us what the marriage license actually represents. I guess that is why they say, "Read the fine print and know what you are signing, before you sign it."

There is not one biblical example of anyone ever needing a "license" or "permission" from any governing body outside the family, until recent history. The only example of permission to marry was simply from the children's parents and most commonly with regard to parents of the Bride.

The right for a man and woman to marry is and will always be, a right given to us by our Father in Heaven, Creator of Heaven and Earth.

It seems crazy to hear a pastor recite; "By the power vested in me by the state of "take your pick," I now pronounce you man and wife." What kind of "power" does the state even have? What are we talking about here? What a bizarre statement to make, if you ask me. It would be more accurately stated, "By the power vested in me by the Living God of Abraham, Isaac and Jacob, I now pronounce you man and wife?" Assuming of course the reader or the couple to be married desire to acknowledge the Living God in the first place.

Marriage has been HIGHJACKED by the government! Something that was once holy has now become reduced to nothing more than a secular contract with the state. The people of God need to return to the idea of holy matrimony and the sanctity of marriage apart from the governmental system via the marriage license. Matrimony is specifically defined as man and woman joining together. Holy is something that is set apart. We need to become set apart from the world governing body for that of the Heavenly governing body.

Problems in Seeking Permission from the State

Being that God created holy matrimony, should not the people of God give acknowledgement, where acknowledgement is due? The state - marriage license gives no acknowledgement to God whatsoever. He is not included or even a thought in the state marriage license or certificate. The Word of God says, "fear of the LORD and depart from evil." What does God think about the idea of a marriage license? Would He consider the marriage license evil? Evil is a strong word, no doubt about it. Let us look at the Merriam Webster definition.

Merriam Webster - definition of "**evil**" is:

Evil[13]: "profoundly immoral and malevolent; harmful or tending to harm…"

So what does evil have to do with the marriage license? Again, why make agreement with an unholy, ungodly, immoral institution that condones unrighteousness such as baby killing (abortion), adultery, condoning homosexual relationships as equal to heterosexual relationships, etc.? What is coming next? The legalization of incest and pedophilia? Each of these things listed and more are

[13] Evil - By permission. From Merriam-Webster's Collegiate® Dictionary, 11th Edition ©2015 by Merriam-Webster, Inc. (www.Merriam-Webster.com)

completely evil, wicked and immoral. Throughout the Bible we see a common theme of God instructing His people to "come out from among them," "...friendship with the world is enmity with God..." and "we are in the world but not of it."

"License" According to Black's Law Dictionary:

License[14]:

1. A revocable permission to commit some act that would otherwise be unlawful. An agreement that it will be lawful for the licensee to enter the licensor's land to do some act that would otherwise be illegal, such as hunting game.

2. The certificate or document evidencing such permission.

Is God Right or the State Right?

By signing a "state marriage license" couples are agreeing that for an adult man and an adult woman, from different families to be married is illegal, without "permission" of the state. In all of history it has never been illegal for men and

[14] License – By permission Black's Law Dictionary, 10th ed. 2014

women to marry. Why admit that an adult male and adult female to marry is unlawful or illegal? Why sign off on something that is not true? It is basically stating, "God you do not know what You are talking about. Marriage is not a good thing. Marriage is an illegal thing. We need to admit it is wrong, then get permission from the government for it to be legitimized and legalized. Otherwise without government permission, we are committing a crime." The idea of marriage being a crime without a license is completely false, untrue and absurd, especially for Bible believers and Jesus followers.

What a complete mockery to the Creator of Heaven, earth and marriage. Signing the marriage license is admits marrying our spouse of the opposite sex, we are doing something that is "criminal", but "*thankfully the state gave us permission to do this illegal act, by granting us license to do so.*"

Double-Minded State

The state seems to have caught a severe case of double-mindedness. In the hour we live, the definition of marriage is under a significant level of scrutiny. Marriage is by definition an exclusive relationship between a man and a woman. Now some small minority of people are attempting to hijack a definition that has been defined since the existence of time. For Christians and Jews for that matter, who follow the Word of God, holy matrimony is at the core foundation of its doctrinal belief system. To erode the definition of marriage, is to erode the very foundation of a people's identity regarding life in the Most High God. While the state may flip flop and flop again on what the definition of marriage is, the believer in Jesus Christ of Nazareth who came in the flesh, need only hold onto what was defined back in the Garden of Eden.

The question needs to be asked in this hour, "If the state can take the ten commandments and prayer out of our school system, then why can't Christians (and heterosexuals for that matter), take their private marriage relationships out of the state?"

The state is swayed by the ever-changing moral compass of mankind's depravity. Christians specifically ought not partner with the double-minded. A house divided will not stand. Such a house is built on sand. When the storm comes, the house will collapse because it was not built upon the Rock.

Fruit of Your Marriage

Trust in the LORD with all your heart, And lean not on your own understanding; In all your ways acknowledge Him, And He shall direct [fn] your paths. Do not be wise in your own eyes; Fear the

LORD and depart from evil.

It will be health to your flesh, [fn] And strength [fn] to your bones. Honor the LORD with your possessions, And with the firstfruits of all your increase; So your barns will be filled with plenty, And your vats will overflow with new wine. – (Proverbs 3:5-10 NKJV)

Check this out, “honor the LORD with your possessions and with the first-fruits of all your increase” – did you know that technically speaking the state owns your "property" and the “fruit of your marriage” which are your children? With a marriage license and birth certificate the children become "wards of the state."

Defining Ward and Guardian from the Black’s Law Dictionary, 10th ed. 2014,

Ward[15]: – A person, usu. A minor, who is under a guardian’s charge or protection. See Guardian

Guardian[16]: – One who has the legal authority and duty to care for another’s person or property, esp. because of the other’s infancy, incapacity, or disability. A guardian may be appointed either for all purposes or for specific purposes.

That is right and the parents are simply guardians or care

---

[15] Ward – By permission Black’s Law Dictionary, 10th ed. 2014
[16] Guardian – By permission Black’s Law Dictionary, 10th ed. 2014

takers of the children. The state is the undisclosed true parent. If the state does not like the way you are raising your children, Child Protective Services (CPS) can legally kidnap your children because of your marriage license and their birth-certificate. In signing the marriage license you instantly give the state which acts through CPS, power and authority over your children.

Some people say, "They can take your kids away anyway without the marriage license if they want." Yes, they can come and attempt to take your children away, but from a legal standpoint, at least without signing the marriage license you are not giving them a leg to stand on. You will have more of a legal foundation to stand on without a marriage license, than you do with one.

Believe it or not there is legal and lawful precedence for several states that prove this reality. The marriage license from a legal standpoint is in fact legal ward of your children. Maybe everything in you is refuting this notion? Technically speaking this is in fact what takes place when couples sign up for the marriage license contract. Signing rights away to the state to be the master of our marriages, owner of our children and yoked to an unholy institution propagating itself, as god and parent. This goes back to the idea of *parens patriae.* There is plenty of case law to support this evidence to be true and factual.

Parens Patriae Case Law

"Ex parte Wright, 225 Ala. 220, 222, 142 So. 672, 674 (1932). See also Fletcher v. Preston, 226 Ala. 665, 148 So. 137 (1933); and Striplin v. Ware, 36 Ala. 87 (1860). In other words, the state is the father and mother of the child and the natural parents are not entitled to custody, except upon the state's beneficent recognition that natural parents presumably will be the best of its citizens to delegate its custodial powers. □ See Chandler v. Whatley, 238 Ala. 206, 208, 189 So. 751, 753 (1939) (quoting Striplin v. Ware, 36 Ala. at 89) ("'The law devolves the custody of infant children upon their parents, not so much upon the ground of natural right in the latter, as because the interests of the children, and the good of the public, will, as a general rule, be thereby promoted.'")."

All of this information is hidden from us and not communicated in a straightforward manner, intentionally. Who would agree to such terms and conditions knowingly? This is the level of ignorance and deception we have been lulled to sleep with by the works of the evil one working through the state corporation. Satan does not play fair. He comes to deceive. He comes to bring bondage.

State Responsibilities and Children

The state is completely responsible for the marriage and its fruit, for example the children and property. The state becomes, once children are born, the legal guardian. People have gone to court battling for their children and have lost. Technically from a legal standpoint, the state, not the parents is the legal guardian and caretaker of the children. *parens patriae* is in effect because the parents have signed these agreements stating one of the three incompetent options spelled out previously.

In a very real sense, the state just became the parent of the husband and wife telling them what they can and cannot do. Do you want God (YHWH) or the state to be your parent telling you how to function within the confines of marriage?

The Burglar Analogy

I liken this to the following analogy:

Signing a marriage license (and birth certificate is included in this) is like going to sleep with your front door unlocked and left wide open. A burglar can simply walk in and take whatever they want anytime.

Without a marriage license and birth certificate, it would be similar to closing your front door and locking it, from a legal standpoint. Yes, you can still get robbed, but at least they are going to have to work a little bit harder by picking a lock, kicking the door in, etc.

Either way anyone is susceptible to being robbed. The question is how much are you going to help the burglar or prevent the burglar from taking your stuff? Such a decision each couple will need to come to a conclusion on.

We live in a world of corruption. In varying degrees the government is corrupt, as well, as its legislation and verdicts. Thankfully, not every lawyer, judge, or jury is corrupt, but we do see injustice come forth in various ways. What else can we expect from a fallen world? Jesus is the only one who can bring perfect justice, which He will, at the end of the age.

Believers in Jesus Christ are waking up to problems of agreement with the state through covenant contracts such as marriage licenses, birth certificates, and the social security program.

Political Agenda Against the Christian Family

It is clear the fix is in. Republican or Democrat, it does not matter. They are all on the same team. The plan is well established. Listen to what one of our state officials said in a radio interview, Senator Peter Hoagland in 1983:

"Fundamental, Bible-believing people do not have the right to indoctrinate their children in their religious beliefs because we, the state, are preparing them for the year 2000, when America will be part of a one-world global society, and their children will not fit in."

Another example why the Bible says, "you are not of this world." Praise the Lord for not fitting into this one-world global society constructed to enslave, imprison and kill, humanity.

"Karl Marx said that in order to establish a perfect socialist state, you have to destroy the family." quoted family psychologist and author John Rosemond. "You have to substitute the government and its authority for parental authority in the rearing of children.[17]"

---

[17] Does your child belong to the state? http://www.wnd.com/2011/11/372409/

These two quotes greatly oppose the Word of God. Secondly, these thoughts and ideas undermine the foundation upon which this nation was created.

The State of Ohio's Statutes: "Terms and Conditions"

Ohio was referenced earlier in this chapter, when looking at Deuteronomy. We see several problems in plain view with the legislation of Ohio. All the states are relatively the same in their statutes regarding the marriage license. Statutes are fairly similar from state to state. Every state should have the statutes (terms and conditions) for marriage license available on their respective governmental website. Most states, if not all, do not offer a printed copy of the terms and conditions with the state marriage license application. This generally means people do not think or know there are any terms and conditions to the marriage adhesion contract, they are about to find themselves involved in.

Word for word from the State of Ohio website indicates:

"Marriage is a legal, as well, as a spiritual and personal relationship. When you state your marriage vows, you enter into a legal contract. There are three parties to that legal contract: 1) you; 2) your spouse; and 3) the state of Ohio. The state is a party to the contract because under its laws, you have certain obligations and responsibilities to each other, to any children you may have, and to the state of Ohio."

As we read in the terms and conditions of the contract, the husband and wife are in fact "married to the state" contractually speaking. The state has complete and total jurisdiction over the marriage, because of the marriage license contract signed by the couple. The couple must comply with all laws established by the government pertaining to their marital relationship without any say. The marriage is instantly and permanently a creature of the state. Included in the terms and conditions as mentioned before is the fact the state also has jurisdiction over the fruit and property of the marriage.

Interesting to note, the state of Ohio defines marriage as three things:

1. Legal Relationship
2. Spiritual Relationship
3. Personal Relationship

We see evidence of the legal relationship, which is the contract. We can see there are personal relationships created between parties or entities; husband, wife and the state of Ohio. Where is God or anything spiritual mentioned after the first sentence? It seems quite clear, it is non-existent. Unless, the state of Ohio sees itself as a god. That would account for the relationship being spiritual, where the husband and wife worship the state by granting it all authority. The state grants permission to marry creating the terms and conditions of the contract. They control the entire nature of the legal relationship. When the officiate says, "By the “power” vested in me by the state of Ohio I now pronounce you husband and wife." we see the spiritual element. The state has set itself up as a god with power to be obeyed, served and granting permission over this marital relationship. The couple has no say in the terms and conditions. The God of the Bible is nowhere to be found or mentioned in the agreement. The couple is completely subject to the state of Ohio as it pertains to any future legalities of the marriage, should something arise.

What about this relationship is spiritual if the husband and wife are atheist or agnostic? Is it possible for something to be “spiritual” for two people, who do not believe in God to begin with? The point is, the state, would be the one making this a spiritual reality in some convoluted way.

Moreover, did you also notice that in the verbiage quoted that it says, "1) you; 2) your spouse; and 3) the state of Ohio." The state does not even define the marriage from a male, female standpoint - husband and wife. They have already set up their legal structure and vocabulary for the doorway of "any" kind of creature based relationship. It is not legal today for anything other than male and female matrimony to be recognized in Ohio (as of April, 2015). The groundwork is already laid, if a day were to arise, where the laws change towards permitting other ungodly defined relationships.

Can we see what is going on here? This is slow and deliberate with the greying of lines; it is all a calculated move with time being the biggest asset.

Illinois Case Law

Let us take a close look at some rulings the state of Illinois determined regarding marriage.

You'll read below various points from Illinois case law:

"When two people decide to get married, they are required to first procure a license from the state. □ If they have children of this marriage, they are required by the state to submit their children to certain things, such as school attendance and vaccinations. □

Furthermore, if at some time in the future the couple decides the marriage is not working, they must petition the state for a divorce. □ Marriage is a three-party contract between the man, the woman, and the state. □Linneman v. Linneman, 1 Ill.App.2d 48, 50, 116 N.E.2d 182, 183 (1953),citing Van Koten v. Van Koten, 323 Ill. 323, 326, 154 N.E. 146 (1926).

The state represents the public interest in the institution of marriage. □Linneman, 1 Ill.App.2d at 50, 116 N.E.2d at 183. □This public interest is what allows the state to intervene in certain situations to protect the interests of members of the family. The *state is like a silent partner* in the family who is not active in the everyday running of the family but becomes active and exercises its power and authority only when necessary to protect some important interest of family life. Taking all of this into consideration, the question no longer is whether the state has an interest or place in disputes such as the one at bar, but it becomes a question of timing and necessity. Has the state intervened too early or perhaps intervened where no intervention was warranted? □ This question then directs our discussion to an analysis of the provision of the Act that allows the challenged state intervention (750 ILCS 5/607(b) (West 1996)).[18]"

[18] See more at: http://caselaw.findlaw.com/il-court-of-appeals/1486817.html#sthash.4KofxrrT.dpuf

1. We see the state of Illinois attempting to "require" a marriage license, when in fact it is illegal for Illinois to "require" anyone to get a marriage license according to the U.S. Constitution and the ruling of the Supreme Court in 1877. By the definition of "fraud", the state of Illinois is committing fraud by making this declaration. We have been lied to, at the state level regarding the issue of the marriage license, plain and simple.

2. Now if a couple does apply for a state marriage license, they are in fact "required" to follow the obligations of the terms and conditions of the agreement with the state in contract with such as vaccinations and school attendance, etc.

3. If the couple wants to end the marriage for one reason or another they must petition the state Corporation to do so.

4. Illinois also communicates like Ohio that the contract is a three way agreement between man, woman and state. Interesting to point out, Illinois makes the clear distinction this agreement is between man, woman and state, unlike Ohio. Yet, ironically, Illinois now recognizes homosexual relationships when a license is issued.

Further Licensing God Given Rights

- What are the long-term implications of the state marriage license?

- What if down the road in the not so distant future, everyone with a marriage license is limited in how many children they are allowed to have?

- What if the state forces people to become sterilized, kill babies or some other practice invading an individual's privacy?

- What if the state corporation begins attempting to license parenthood?

This is an absurd thought because we know everyone has the God given right to have children and it is perfectly legal under the United States Constitution. Yet, that is exactly what is going on right now with marriage! The control is escalating day by day. If the state changes the terms and conditions of the agreement, the nuclear family could begin to look even more skewed from God's original design. We the people are on a slippery slope regarding the legalities of marriage and family in the United States of America. The law shapes the constructs of what family looks like with significant implications; should we continue in this direction as a nation or even as individuals? I hope not.

"The state is like a silent partner in the family..." and "becomes active and exercises its power and authority only when necessary to protect some important interest of family life." This statement is where some in the Christian community make the claim that the marriage license and involvement of the state creates a "polygamous" relationship from a legal stand-point because the state is a silent "partner." No thank you. The marriage partners need only be the husband, wife and the Living God.

A Word from Hosea

1 Hear the word of the LORD, You children of Israel, For the LORD [brings] a charge against the inhabitants of the land: "There is no truth or mercy Or knowledge of God in the land.

2 [By] swearing and lying, Killing and stealing and committing adultery, They break all restraint, With bloodshed upon bloodshed.

3 Therefore the land will mourn; And everyone who dwells there will waste away With the beasts of the field And the birds of the air; Even the fish of the sea will be taken away.

4 "Now let no man contend, or rebuke another; For your people [are] like those who contend with the priest.

5 Therefore you shall stumble in the day; The prophet also shall stumble with you in the night; And I will destroy your mother.

6 My people are destroyed for lack of knowledge. Because you have rejected knowledge, I also will reject you from being priest for Me; Because you have forgotten the law of your God, I also will forget your children.

7 "The more they increased, The more they sinned against Me; I will change their glory into shame.

8 They eat up the sin of My people; They set their heart on their iniquity.

9 And it shall be: like people, like priest. So I will punish them for their ways, And reward them for their deeds.

10 For they shall eat, but not have enough; They shall commit harlotry, but not increase; Because they have ceased obeying the LORD. (Hosea 4:1-10 NKJV)

For those of us who believe in Jesus, we can see this to be

true in our land. How the people have broken restraint because we have left our first love, Jesus, and the Word of God. The reality is there is so much to be aware of we lack knowledge in the fundamental things of life. It does not help that we have been lied to and deceived into believing one thing when it is not even true. Let us return to the Living God of Abraham, Isaac and Jacob and do things His way. He is merciful and will forgive us as we seek Him out in humility. He is faithful to heal and restore us.

Prayer

Father, may we not be the people Hosea speaks about. Turn our hearts away from blind ignorance. Let the laws, statutes and precepts of this nation be established upon righteousness. Let Your justice pour out from Heaven. Let the lies and deception flowing from all world governmental systems stop right now in Jesus name. Turn our hearts towards the things that matter to You. Let us see the folly and error of our ways, so as to turn from them. Expose the ignorance and let the Truth connect to our hearts. Let us not be wise in our own eyes. Cast down the gross pride and arrogance of this nation. Let us be a people that seek to walk in humility, rather than by being humbled because of how we take pride in sinning before You. May we be a people that move into righteousness, holiness, and justice for the Living God according to Your ways. Holy Spirit, I ask that You bring revelation and light to this topic. I ask You to speak to the hearts of Your people, so the bold Truth will rise and everything else be burned. Let Your Word speak. May the Holy Spirit of God give us, His people, greater revelation as to how to walk the earth in this hour. How to stand against an unrighteous governing body that is in direct opposition to the things of a Holy God. May we enter into the sufferings of Christ according to righteousness. Father, thank You that You are strong enough to save us; Your children. In Y'shua's (Jesus') name. Thank You.

Then the Lord answered me and said: Write the vision And make it plain on tablets, That he may run who reads it. (Habakkuk 2:2 NKJV)

5

ADHESION CONTRACT

Last chapter we briefly brought up the idea of the marriage license being an adhesion contract. So what is an adhesion contract? Let us take a closer look at Black's Dictionary.

Adhesion Contract[19]:

"A standard-form contract prepared by one party, to be signed by the party in a weaker position, usu. A consumer, who has little choice about the terms. – Also termed contract of adhesion; adhesory contract; adhesionary contract; take-it-or-leave-it contract; leonine contract."

Adhesion Contract - For a contract to be treated as a contract of adhesion, it must be presented on a standard form on a "take it or leave it" basis, and give one party no

[19] Adhesion Contract – By permission Black's Law Dictionary, 10th ed. 2014

ability to negotiate because of their unequal position. Notice how the definition uses the word, "consumer." This word choice lends itself to the idea that the state is a corporation "selling" a product or service to a "consumer." The state clearly has a primary focus of control tied to revenue generation, simply by offering such a contract to begin with.

Some examples of everyday adhesion contracts would be the following:

Social Security Numbers

Driver's Licenses

Birth Certificates

Cell Phone Contracts

Cable TV Contracts

Online Agreements

The list goes on, but you get an idea as to how one identifies the adhesion contract. All of these contracts are on a voluntary basis.

Taking a Closer Look

Let us look at the nature of the contract itself. The state marriage license is in fact a 3-way secular adhesion contract (or covenant) between you, your spouse and the state. The state is the principal in your secular marriage contract. The husband and wife are secondary parties; subject to whatever the state legislates as law without any say.

This document is dynamic and subject to change at the whims of the state. The husband and wife have no voice or argument in the matter. Rarely, if ever, are couples provided the terms and conditions regarding the "voluntary" state marriage license. Most people are not aware these terms and conditions even exist. The state completely fails to communicate or offer these terms and conditions in writing, when providing the state License itself.

One could argue this is not a true contract. A contract must be entered into knowingly, understandably, intentionally and fully informed. Without such knowledge, understanding and aptitude, technically there can be no contract. I refer to such actions as “designed ignorance” on the state’s part. Apparently, there are no "lemon" laws when dealing with the state's "sales" integrity or lack there of. Ignorance is a huge asset to any sales process. The less the customer knows, the more likely the company with a sales proposition has to close the transaction in their favor. What makes matters worse is the fact the state keeps the employees ignorant as well. After calling several states and speaking with countless people, it is clear – ignorance is the plan. Nobody can give a straight answer. The state benefits in keeping both their employees and the unsuspecting couple in the dark as to the details of this contract. Remember back to the meeting in 1911, where the state's goal was to "*abolish common law marriage.*" Achieving this goal, means revenue generation year after year via the fees associated with the state License, not to mention bigger revenues on the back end of divorce. The state cannot make any money off of a "common law" or "biblical" marriage.

When the couple provides payment for the licensing fee, "consideration" takes place, communicating the establishment of a covenant. Signing and paying for a license, instantly establishes agreement between the three parties. All of the state's statutes, rules and regulations become active in this relationship instantly.

Do you notice how much of a parallel the state and businesses are in the preceding paragraphs? It is time to shift our thinking of government. Government has become a business rather than an institution seeking the good of the people, as it was originally intended to be. The nation was founded on the idea of a "government for the people by the people," but now there is much more at play in our government's motivation.

In researching the definition of the adhesion contract and reviewing court law there is one document that really "nails the hammer on the head" regarding the "business" proposition of the marriage license. The document is called, "Challenging Adhesion Contracts in California: A *Consumer's* Guide." The entire document is about defining what kind of contracts businesses can present to consumers. The adhesion contract makes it possible for "business" to take place. Businesses add all kinds of terms and conditions so as to advantage themselves against any harm or responsibility for wrong doing towards the consumer. The document is quite revealing as to how corrupt businesses can become because the consumer signs off on the particular service contract. The only problem with the government adhesion contract is, who is watching the government to prevent them from taking advantage of citizens? Aside from God, it does not appear that there is any other agency watching to ensure justice for the citizens.

Look at the Terms and Conditions

As much as we Christians want to tell ourselves God is a part of the state marriage license covenant, He is not. He has zero to do with this "voluntary" adhesion contract. God is not considered, mentioned or welcomed in any capacity. He is not named anywhere in the terms, conditions or paperwork.

Here are some questions we need to be asking ourselves as it pertains to marriage and the state's involvement:

- Since when did marriage become a business proposition with a state institution?

- Isn't marriage simply about defining a private "relational status" between two people?

- How can God be a part of any contract that He is

not even mentioned in?

- What are we to do about this current reality?

6

THE FRAUD MATTER

As previously discussed, marriage and family are one of the most, if not the most important elements of any society. God established society through the sanctity of marriage. Without man and woman coming together in the confines of marriage, society would completely fail to exist as God intended. The holy union of man and woman was one of, if not the first blessing God gave to humanity.

In the United States of America marriage is clearly under attack on all sides. In fact, broken marriages are a global issue. This is not new information. The news, movies, TV shows, music, all communicate this fact loud and clear. The question is, "Why is this happening?" Part of the reason is because the government is making laws and regulations promoting the degradation of marriage and beyond that, the family unit. Another reason is that the government has attempted to replace God in every sense.

The United States of America, founded upon Christian principles, leads the world in the amount of divorces that take place every single year. Yes, the United States of America is number 1, when it comes to the divorce rate. Wikipedia says that 60-76% of Americans claim to be Christian. These are sobering statistics.

Christians who are "born again" and seeking the Kingdom of God and His righteousness ought not experience the pain of divorce. So why are we? There are a number of areas we can look to because it is a complex issue. I mention the stats on divorce, not to condemn those who have experienced such painful loss, but to point out the issue. Why is it so tough for our marriages to stay together today? There has got to be more going on here than meets the eye! It was not always like this, as we look at the words of Jesus.

Jesus said to them, "Moses, because of the hardness of your hearts, permitted you to divorce your wives, but from the beginning it was not so. – (Matthew 19:8 NKJV)

What are we participating in that we "think" or even better, "believe" are righteous acts and are not? Such a question is a huge can of worms. For the purposes of this book, we are focusing on the "voluntary" marriage license.

The state government has committed fraud by concealing the truth against its citizens. Now, you might be saying to yourself, "Wow! Those are strong words. Fraud? Really? I do not know that I believe that..."

Fraud[20]:1. A knowing misrepresentation or knowing concealment of a material fact made to induce another to act to his or her detriment. • Fraud is usu. a tort, but in some cases (esp. when the conduct is willful) it may be a crime. — Also termed intentional fraud.

2. A reckless misrepresentation made without justified belief in its truth to induce another person to act.

3. A tort arising from a knowing or reckless misrepresentation or concealment of material fact made to induce another to act to his or her detriment. • Additional elements in a claim for fraud may include reasonable reliance on the misrepresentation and damages resulting from this reliance.

4. Unconscionable dealing; esp., in contract law, the unfair use of the power arising out of the parties' relative positions and resulting in an unconscionable bargain. See defraud. — fraudulent, adj.

---

[20] Fraud – By permission Black's Law Dictionary, 10th ed. 2014

Illinois Website on Marriage License

Here is one example taking place against the American people. Illinois on their website has the following statement:

"Before getting married in Chicago or suburban Cook County, couples **must** obtain a marriage license from the Cook County Clerk's office."

Merriam Webster's definition of "must"

Must[21]: 1 *a* : **be commanded or requested to** <you *must* stop> *b* : be urged to : ought by all means to <you *must* read that book>

2: be compelled by physical necessity to <one *must* eat to live> : be required by immediate or future need or purpose to <we *must* hurry to catch the bus>

3*a* : be obliged to : be compelled by social considerations to <I *must* say you're looking well> b : **be required by law, custom, or moral conscience to** <we *must* obey the rules> *c* : be determined to <if you *must* go at least wait for me> d : be unreasonably or perversely compelled to <why *must* you argue>

[21] Must - By permission. From Merriam-Webster's Collegiate® Dictionary, 11th Edition ©2015 by Merriam-Webster, Inc. (www.Merriam-Webster.com).

4: be logically inferred or supposed to <it *must* be time>

5: be compelled by fate or by natural law to <what *must* be will be>

6: was or were presumably certain to : was or were bound to <if he did it she *must* have known>

7*dial*: may, shall —used chiefly in questions

This is based on the fact the United States Supreme Court has ruled AGAINST the state's making the marriage license mandatory.

Here is where things get a little sticky. Notice how there are multiple meanings and definitions for one word. How do we know which one to use? The definitions of words are how a society is able to accurately and justly give out court rulings. In the Black's Law Dictionary the word "must" is defined with the synonym words - "may and shall."

The lawyers are veiling the true intention or realities of your rights. While the common individual thinks of the Merriam Webster definition "required by law" perspective, the legal definition is what is important. The word "may" is also interchangeably used with the word "must." So what seems like fraud from the outset based upon common law, has become a matter of semantics and definition of choice. The lawyers know full-well how to ride the razors edge in this game of cat and mouse. We the people need to become educated, rightly, so as to avoid this game all together. All of this, wording and definitions are used in a shrewd manner so the state corporation can "close the sale" over and over and over again.

In the Illinois example the word, "may" can be interchanged with the word "must." The slight difference is quite substantial because "may" is optional in our thinking, while "must" comes across as mandatory. All of this wording is used to prod people into the marriage license adhesion contract. Yet in case law we looked at earlier, they go so far as to use the word require.

Take a Look at the U.S. Supreme Court Ruling

96 U.S. 76 - 24 L.Ed. 826 MEISTER v. MOORE October Term, 1877

"No doubt, a statute may take away a common-law right; but there is always a presumption that the legislature has no such intention, unless it be plainly expressed. A statute may declare that no marriages shall be valid unless they are solemnized in a prescribed manner; but such an enactment is a very different thing from a law requiring all marriages to be entered into in the presence of a magistrate or a clergyman, or that it be preceded by a license, or publication of banns, or be attested by witnesses. *Such formal provisions may be construed as merely directory, instead of being treated as destructive of a common-law right to form the marriage relation by words of present assent.* And such, we think, has been the rule generally adopted in construing statutes regulating marriage."

Essentially, the state wants the people to believe we "must" (from the Merriam Webster definition - required by law) apply for or obtain a state marriage license and certificate, while hiding behind the (Black's Law definition - may) the Federal Court system ruled the license is "merely directory." If people want to "voluntarily" sign this piece of paper from the state to have their marriage "recognized" then they may do so. Not having signed any such paper from any state is quite alright, assuming some fundamental principles are followed to "prove" your marriage. This topic will be discussed further in a later chapter.

Over the years, the state government has become very good at propagating the supposed requirement of a state issued marriage license and certificate. Nothing could be further from the truth. The United States Constitution is founded upon common-law principles that can only be surrendered at the "consent" or "volunteering" of the individual. Matrimony is a contract and relational status of an adult man and woman. The state does not have any business being involved, unless otherwise invited.

7

LAWS OF THE LAND

At this point we know, the marriage license is completely "voluntary." *No one is forcing us to sign the license.* No government will make a couple register their marriage with the state. We choose to do this voluntarily.

The United States Constitution

Now what about obeying the laws and ordinances of the land? I am all for it!

The 1st amendment of the Constitution of the United States of America reads:

"Congress shall make no law respecting an establishment of religion, or prohibiting the free exercise thereof; or abridging the freedom of speech, or of the press; or the right of the people peaceably to assemble, and to petition the Government for a redress of grievances."

Freedom to Practice Religion

This is to address the Romans 13 argument. We must realize the founders of this Republic (the United States of America) put the Word of God above any and all man's laws. In fact, the laws of the land are subject to the Bible first and foremost because of the 1st amendment right of the United States Constitution. The only way the rights do not take affect is if we the people give them up by signing them away or do not follow the Word of God. In signing your marriage license you "give up" your God given right in exchange for a "privilege" of the state. Keep in mind, a privilege can be revoked or changed at any point. A "right" is unshakeable. Hold onto your God given right!

What is also noteworthy is the idea that the absolute legal authority of the United States of America is the Constitution. The President, Congress and Supreme Court are all subject to this authority - the law of the land. The first amendment of the United States of America's Constitution is the idea of "freedom of religion and freedom of speech." If the religious doctrine I follow indicates that I can be married without a marriage license, then in a very real sense of the law, I can be legally married with a valid, legal, lawful marriage.

We the people must hold onto God-given rights. It is time to take a stand. Please say, “NO” to the marriage license. Let us give our marriages and families back to God!

The U.S. Supreme Court Defines "Liberty"

“In 1923 the U.S. Supreme Court defined "liberty" as the right to, "marry, establish a home and bring up children…"

MEYER vs. STATE OF NEBRASKA, 262 U.S. 390 (1923)

'No state ... shall deprive any person of life, liberty or property without due process of law.'

While this court has not attempted to define with exactness the liberty thus guaranteed, the term has received much consideration and some of the included things have been definitely stated. Without doubt, it denotes not merely freedom from bodily restraint but also the right of the individual to contract, to engage in any of the common occupations of life, to acquire useful knowledge, to marry, establish a home and bring up children, to worship God according to the dictates of his own conscience, and generally to enjoy those privileges long recognized at common law as essential to the orderly pursuit of happiness by free men.)”

For those of you reading this that are currently in a

marriage license or have had one in the past, take hope. Remember James 4:6, stay in a place of peace because "He gives more grace." Chances are you did not question any of this and did not know the ramifications in the marriage license. *There is a deliberate deception taking place upon the people.* The good news is, people are beginning to stand against this unrighteous tyranny.

Realize, we are under attack by the evil one, through the tool of the government.

Be sober, be vigilant; because your adversary the devil walks about like a roaring lion, seeking whom he may devour. (1 Peter 5:8 NKJV)

Licenses are Designed to Deny People

The reason *any* license throughout history has been instituted was so that the power of "denial" could exist. In the mid-1800s, if a county or state didn't want inter-racial marriages, they could simply deny the license. If whites and blacks didn't obtain a marriage license, further consequence could ensue. Eventually in 1923, the "Uniform Marriage and Marriage License Act" was passed by the federal government – 6 years later, marriage licenses were being distributed in every state to ALL people, including interracial couples. Marriage had now become a government institution.

Marriage licenses in the USA have only existed on any significant scale since 1929. Most marriages, other than inter-racial marriages, before this change, never included a marriage license. Marriage throughout the world was and is a fundamental right to unite with members of the opposite sex.

ARTICLE ISection 10. [1] No state shall enter into any treaty, alliance, or confederation; grant letters of marque and reprisal; coin money; emit bills of credit; make any thing but gold and silver coin a tender in payment of debts; pass any bill of attainder, **ex-post-facto law**, or law impairing the obligation of contract; or grant any title of nobility.

Declaration of Independence – In Congress, July 4, 1776

The unanimous Declaration of the thirteen United States of America,

Excerpt,"We hold these truths to be self-evident, that all men are created equal, that they are endowed by their Creator with certain inalienable Rights, that among these are Life, Liberty and the pursuit of Happiness.---"

Our government began with the idea of freedom. Every man had inalienable rights – Life, Liberty and the pursuit of Happiness. Marriage is one of these inalienable rights.

Life, human life comes about righteously when an adult male and adult female come together in holy matrimony. Men and women have the freedom and right to be lawfully married without permission or contract from a state institution. Marriage is something that, for the believer, is between God, the man and the woman. How is holy matrimony to take place within the state institution that denies the very existence of a Creator?

It is highly advisable not to be yoked, in a covenant so vital as holy matrimony lasting to the end of one's life, with the state. Somehow we have been blinded to these realities? All too often we see examples of Christian couples part taking in the state license. The Church is waking up. Can holy matrimony truly exist if the state is a silent partner to the marriage? Jesus did not redeem the state, die for the state or have any part in the state government's covenant – ie license. His government and this world government function separate from one another. It is time discern between the holy and unholy, the clean and unclean. Shall we exit the world drowning in delusion, to find refuge in the "ark of the covenant" found alone in holy matrimony?

8

SOLUTIONS FOR A LEGAL MARRIAGE, WITHOUT A MARRIAGE LICENSE

One of the big questions to address in this book is, can a man and woman be married legally without a state marriage license in the USA?

Whether we realize it or not, there are multiple options for a couple to define their marriage relationship from a legal standpoint. The most practiced option is the Civil or Statutory Marriage license and certificate issued by the state.

A less popular method used about a hundred years ago was what is known as "common law marriage." states have worked hard to cover up and sweep this option under the rug. It is very much a legitimate method in which people today in 2015 can enter into holy matrimony, without the state. Let us take a closer look as to the history and context for which Common Law marriage functions. "biblical Marriage" would fall under the category of "common law marriage" in the eyes of the state.

What are our options regarding legal marriage in the United states of America? Remember, George Washington, Abraham Lincoln and Thomas Jefferson were all married without a marriage license.

Common Law and Marriage

So you might be asking yourself, "What exactly is "common law marriage?"

Common Law[22]: The body of law derived from judicial decisions, rather than from statutes or constitutions.

Common law marriage is used throughout history because it is every man and woman's right to be married, as we learned earlier. All marriage does is communicates a change in status relationally. Where common law comes

[22] Common Law – By permission Black's Law Dictionary, 10th ed. 2014

into play is determining which people are husband and wife and which people are simply involved in another type of a relationship outside the confines of marriage. How do we know conclusively who is married and who is not? The reason for properly defining the relationship is the possibility of the legal ramifications down the road. For example if there should be an unfortunate death, who receives or inherits the property of the individual who passed away? What if there's a medical emergency and only the family can see the individual in the hospital? Defining the relationship openly and broadly helps bring forth the evidence necessary for situations that may arise.

The only time it is necessary for the law to get involved regarding a marriage, is in the case where the validity is in question. Using prior case law helps determine the relational status in question as to whether or not a marriage is truly established. As in the example of a spouse passing away, it is necessary to determine if the couple was married before the death occurred.

Is Common Law and Biblical Marriage Legal?

Common law marriage is defined by the body of law derived from judicial decisions, rather than from statutes or constitutions, case law. Meaning, we look at previous cases to determine how to identify what marriage is and is not.

Since the Supreme Court case of Meister vs. Moore in 1877, the ruling we looked at in previous chapters highlights two things:

1. Marriage is a common right.
2. A marriage license is merely directory or in other words voluntary.

Common law marriage is lawful and legal. The popular misconception of "common law marriage" is that people tend to think it is not legal, when in fact it is totally 100% legal. Common law marriage is simply not "recognized" by most of the states, but it is legal in all 50 states. Let that sink in for a moment. Read it out loud a couple of times and meditate on this truth. We have been so indoctrinated it can take multiple times reading this information for the truth to take hold within us.

Statutory or (Civil) Law[23]: 2. The body of law imposed by the state, as opposed to moral law. 3. The law of civil or private rights, as opposed to criminal law or administrative law.

Common Law[24]: The body of law derived from judicial

[23] Statutory – By permission Black's Law Dictionary, 10th ed. 2014
[24] Common Law – By permission Black's Law Dictionary, 10th ed. 2014

decisions, rather than from statutes or constitutions.

Directory Requirement[25]: A statutory or contractual instruction to act in a way that is advisable, but not absolutely essential — in contrast to a mandatory requirement. • A directory requirement is frequently introduced by the word should or, less frequently, shall (which is more typically a mandatory word).

As discussed, the issue is not whether common law or biblical marriage is "legal" it is simply a question as to whether or not it is "recognized" by a particular state. The reason it is not recognized is because the state has nothing to do with the contract of common law or biblical marriage. Since the state is "left out" of the covenant/contract completely, they do not know anything about the "terms and conditions" and are not even a party to the contract. Thus it is not "recognized" by the state. Similarly to how God is left out of the state license covenant, the state is left out of the biblical or common law covenant. Understand, there is a distinct difference between "unlawful" and "recognized." We need to identify and discern the differences between the two ideas.

"Civil or statutory marriage" is registered with the state,

---

[25] Directory Requirement – By permission Black's Law Dictionary, 10th ed. 2014

which includes a 3 party adhesion agreement between state, husband and wife or a 3 party agreement between the state and two homosexuals, depending on the state in question. The state is part of this marriage license contract, thus keeping track of such records. Due to the fact the state is part of the "civil or statutory marriage" there are terms and conditions the state is suppose to provide each couple, making them known, therefore causing it to be recognized.

Any marriage not "recognized" by the state, does not automatically mean it would be an "invalid or illegal" marriage. Common law marriage, which would include biblical marriage, is legal in every state. Common law marriage is "valid" and legal in every state in the union; it simply may not be "recognized" by every state in the union, simply because the terms and conditions are unknown.

Identifying a Common Law or Biblical Marriage

What does the court use to identify the validity of a marriage or not? They use jurisprudence, in other words previous case law. There are questions the court will ask the couple to prove their marriage.

Some of the following questions the court will ask include:

1. Is there any kind of verifiable contract - oral or

written that currently exists?

Verbal agreements do stand up in a court of law to validate a marriage. However, if one spouse dies then proving the verbal agreement outside of witnesses could be difficult to prove. It is highly advised to develop a written agreement signed by both husband and wife.

The family Bible can also be signed as a legal marriage contract valid in a court of law. This was commonly practiced less than a hundred years ago.

2. Is there a marriage contract in the future or presently?

A written marriage contract needs to establish the marriage in present tense, rather than some arbitrary future date in time. With that being said, the court system has supported future tense marriage agreements. Keep in mind even though courts have supported future tense marriage, such an agreement is by no means as secure as a present tense contract. Such marriage contracts are best written to communicate the fundamental rights and duties of the parties involved.

3. Has a wedding ceremony or solemnization taken

place?

A religious wedding ceremony is no longer necessary to the court when determining and identifying a marriage. The reason for this is due to the fact that agnostics and atheists would not be seen as having a valid marriage if this were still an issue. The irony of agnostics and atheists marrying is that it is fundamentally Christian and God centric. These groups may still have a ceremony; it need not be "religious" in nature for the wedding and marriage to be established in a court of law.

4. Did any religious figure perform the ceremony?

While it is an indicator that a "wedding" took place, it's not necessary to have someone perform a ceremony in order for the couple to be seen as married. Lawfully, Adam and Eve and Isaac and Rebecca's examples are two wedding examples that highlight this reality. The only individual responsible for performing a ceremony in those cases would have been God Himself.

5. Were there witnesses to the ceremony or solemnization?

This element is helpful in creating the argument for a valid marriage as well, because it is public and has an amount of witnesses to verify that a wedding took place and a marriage was formed. Remember, a ceremony simply offers more credibility to the evidence of a marital relationship being established.

6. Has cohabitation taken place?

Consummation and cohabitation play a role in the evidence of a marriage being established. Isaac and Rebecca basically met and went right into his mother's tent to consummate the marriage. From that point on, the two were married and Isaac loved his wife. The court system takes this relational element into account.

7. Did the couple make a marriage certificate to solemnize the day their marriage began?

A certificate of marriage can be created on your own. Hire someone to make one or simply use the family Bible. You will want to fill out the certificate with dates, names, and even the location the wedding or agreement took place. Have the certificate signed by the husband and wife, along with three other witnesses such as a pastor and a couple family members. Ultimately the signature of three other witnesses will communicate the agreement of the husband

and wife's marital status.

When a couple memorializes the event, ceremony, solemnization this can be used in court as evidence that there is in fact a marriage relationship in place that is valid.

8. Was there a secret marriage?

Sometimes it is necessary for a couple to have a "secret" marriage. In such cases, the court has ruled these type of marriages, valid and legal. Secret marriages are more challenging to prove and therefore it is advised to make the marriage relationship public.

9. Are there any previous marriages in place before the marriage in question?

Before a couple can get married, any prior marriages must be filed through the court system properly from a legal standpoint. The court in most cases will not recognize a relationship as a marriage, if there's a pre-existing legal marriage in place. If both parties have never been married before then there's no issue to be concerned with on this point.

10. Is the marriage based on false information?

If two people join together and one person has falsified their identity, the validity of the marriage could very well be in question. The court will deal with such scenarios on a case-by-case basis.

Looking at the Entire Scope of the Relationship

The judicial system generally looks at the overall scope of the couple's relationship with key elements to be identified as defining marriage or not. If you are sincere in your intentions to marry, make it as plain as day for anybody to look at your relationship and say, "Of course they're married." Obviously, there are varying needs and circumstances as to how or why people portray themselves in a certain light. Simply attempt to follow some of the guiding fundamentals and you will be all right.

Exploring a historical perspective of common law or biblical marriage there are several indicators that define a marriage. Examining further, here is a list of things the court will use as evidence or markers to rule a relational status is in fact a marriage relationship:

- Parental Consent

- Public Notice - before the wedding ceremony

- Wedding Ceremony - while a public traditional wedding ceremony is very helpful in proving the common law marriage, it is in fact quite alright to NOT have a ceremony or a religious figure marry the couple. We know that common law is based upon the Bible and therefore nowhere in Scripture does it command or require the permission of a religious leader to perform a ceremony. There is court precedence that backs this view and position perfectly.

- Wedding Guest Book - conveys a list of people who can testify to solemnization.

- Marriage Contract - verbal or written agreement of the male and female. For example, two people verbally agreeing to marry each other or signing the family Bible would qualify as a written agreement.

- Certificate of Marriage - signed by officiate, husband, wife, and two other witnesses. A document of this kind is in fact considered a legal record, which makes the common law marriage both legal and lawful. This document could be registered, as well, with the County Clerk or Registrar. With a certified copy of the original notice, this could be presented as if it were a marriage license. In law, your certificate may have more authority than that of a marriage license.

- Memorialize the Wedding - with pictures and video documentation.

- Cohabitation - Once verbal or written agreements are signed and you are officially married, begin cohabitating together.

- Public Reference - refer to one another as husband and wife.

The purpose of this chapter is to lay out legal options for those hoping to get married without direct government involvement. For those concerned about what Romans 13 and 1 Peter speak to regarding obeying authorities your conscience can be clear on all counts. Basically prove a legal marriage in a court of law - legally and lawfully by laying out the evidences mentioned above.

Common Law for Biblical Marriage

Common law and more specifically biblical marriage give honest, sincere Christians a real viable marriage option. Is it less popular today, than a marriage license? Yes. Any less valid? No. This is not an unlawful approach to justify any type of sin. Individual men and women are legally able to marry, without being yoked to the state government through adhesion contract.

The Word of God is holy. God is looking for a people set apart to Him. Common law comes from the Bible and should promote a greater level of commitment, with God's favor and blessing. Biblical, common law marriage must be taken seriously, joyfully, and deserves real attention. Covenant lasts a lifetime.

Reasons for Proving Marriage

A couple might be asked to prove the validity of their marriage. Some reasons may include receiving rights or benefits unavailable to singles. Examples of this are life insurance, medical benefits, death benefits, etc. Generally speaking, if a business is asking for proof of marriage, a notarized or properly executed marriage certificate ought to suffice. In the event such evidence is unsatisfactory, a sworn affidavit ought to work out. The only time the affidavit will not work, is when the opposing party rebuts the affidavit.

For a government agency, challenging the validity of your marriage, submit the marriage certificate. If any particular business or corporation is not satisfied with the marriage certificate, ask for an "administrative hearing."

Should a hearing be required, some tips to follow:

- Provide evidence of marriage agreement, certificate and memorialized evidence such as guest book, pictures, and/or video of the wedding.

- Testify about the reality of your marriage: living together, having kids, call each other husband and wife. Site the Meister vs. Moore case that state marriage statutes/licenses are merely directory in nature. There cannot be any adverse consequence or invalidation for not following a statute which is only directory.

- Ask the agency representative (who should not be the hearing officer) to be sworn in. Then ask him or her to enter into the official record any evidence the agency possesses invalidating your common law marriage.

Show up prepared and chances are likely, the court will rule in your favor. If not, you can take it to an appeals court and provide the same evidence where the court will eventually rule in favor of your marriage.

Moving Forward with a Hearing

Collect all your evidence as mentioned above for proving your marriage.

If you are sworn in, you and your spouse can communicate you are married to each other. Always reference the Meister vs. Moore case, while giving testimony as well.

You are also able to ask the government representative (not the hearing officer) to be sworn in, requesting any evidence conveying that your marriage is invalid. Should court action be necessary, you can then take the hearing evidence and use it in court. Have the agency enter into the official record, all evidence they have, to prove your marriage is invalid.

Go to the hearing with your communication points well prepared. The governmental agency will likely recognize your marriage as legal, valid and binding. If for some reason, they do not see things that way, then the official record of this hearing can be used against them in court.

What About Fake and False Marriage Arrangements?

In a fallen world, with sinful humanity, there is going to be corruption. Marriage is no exception to this reality. Occasionally we hear about people claiming to be married, that are not. This can happen with a state marriage license (statutory marriage) or a biblical marriage (judicial law). An example of this is when people pretend to be married to gain citizenship in a particular country. A foreigner, paying a United States citizen a sum of money, to become a citizen through "marriage" happens fairly regularly. Human nature is predisposed to abusing laws and common law marriage is no exception.

People will continue to misrepresent themselves and the nature of a relationship. It should be no surprise to you that this will continue until heaven and earth pass away. The judicial system has established guideposts to accurately determine the validity of a marriage, under common law.

Without question, people who are genuinely interested in establishing a life-long committed marriage, ought to use their right to "common law" and biblical matrimony. Marriage is holy in the eyes of God and is nothing to be taken lightly. Marriage must be handled with reverence, remain undefiled and something where two people are set apart unto each other, the rest of their life.

What about the Children Under 18?

Every marriage is centered on an agreement or contract, whether it is common law or statutory law.

In dealing with such matters there are two options:

1. Go to the statutory court; subject your marriage to their rules and regulations. The court has no problem taking your money and telling you how to run your family. As soon as you take your marriage and family to the court system's jurisdiction, from that point on, the family is under the court's supervision, dictates and rulings. No questions asked, no rebuttals. It is their way or the highway. Also, keep in mind that the children and property become the state’s once you put yourself under their body of law. This is mentioned and discussed in prior chapters.

2. Write out a covenant before marriage. Communicate each other's roles, wishes, desires and expectations for marriage. This statement is true, "If you love me, you will put it in writing." If you love someone, you want to look out for his or her best interests. Write out what each other expects, anticipates and is hoping for in marriage. Putting expectations on the table, in written form, helps increase understanding for the couple.

A significant reason couples choose common law marriage is so they can be adults determining the nature of their private, personal relationship. The state has no business butting in on holy matrimony.

States "Recognizing" Common Law Marriage

As of December 2014, communicated below is a list of states that currently “recognize” common law marriage. Remember, “recognize” and “lawful” are two different things. Common law marriage is “lawful” and “legal” in all fifty states. A number of states simply do not “recognize” the marriage, because they are not a part of the contractual agreement, such as the marriage license.

Common law “recognized” states:

Alabama

Colorado

District of ColumbiaGeorgia (if created before 1/1/97)

Idaho (if created before 1/1/96)

Iowa

Kansas

Montana

New Hampshire (for inheritance purposes only)

New Mexico

Ohio (if created before 10/10/91)

Oklahoma (possibly only if created before 11/1/98) Oklahoma's laws and court decisions may be in conflict about whether common law marriages formed in that state after 11/1/98 will be recognized.)

Pennsylvania (if created before 1/1/05)

Rhode Island

South Carolina

Texas

Utah

9

HOW CAN I GET OUT?

How can one get out of the marriage license relationship with the state?

There are at least two possible options regarding leaving the state marriage license.

1. Take the state to court for not providing you with the terms and conditions of the marriage license. According to contract law, there cannot be a valid signature, if the signee has not been provided full disclosure when the agreement is presented. The terms and conditions should be provided to any individual in conjunction with the contract. If you were not provided such information, then the contract can be voided, because there was not proper consideration before signing. Talk with a contract lawyer regarding your options as to voiding your marriage license.

2. The other option is to visit the family court and "divorce the state." Indicating to the court you are divorcing and dissolving the relationship legally. The overall idea is to keep the marriage together in the eyes of God and each other, not actually dissolving the marriage. To the state it will look like you were divorced. Become remarried in the eyes of God, without the marriage license in front of friends, family, or witnesses. Have a new wedding ceremony, even if it is only in front of three other people or a small number of people. In a court of law, you will be able to prove a marriage exists.

This book is in no way giving legal advice or legal council as to how any individual or couple is to proceed in this issue of the marriage license. Each couple needs to determine what is best for their relationship and it is advised you speak with a lawyer. There are so many dynamics that take place in such situations. Only the married couple would be able to determine the best route, with the idea of dissolving the contract with the state. To suggest divorcing the state has profound implications. Things to consider are the unity of the marriage, the health of the marriage, and any children under 18 would cause additional challenges from the court system. These are all just a few examples. Ultimately, as Christians, get educated on the legalities, read the Word of God, pray about it and respond to what the Holy Spirit reveals to you as a couple.

If there are dependent children involved, consider waiting until they are 18 before divorcing the state. Otherwise, you come under the state's statutes in family court. The state will tell you what your parameters for visitation will be, etc. The time to test the waters for divorcing the state, are ideal, before having children or after all your children are 18. Again, these are simply suggestions as viable options and things to be aware of in such matters.

Whatever the solution or direction a couple proceeds in, unity is a key element. Please seek council and talk with whomever you need to best determine solutions that may work for you specifically.

Depending on which state you live in things will play out uniquely to that body of law. I strongly encourage you to do your own homework and a thorough investigation. Today, each state generally has a website with statutes for the marriage license, including dissolution processes.

Implications of the State Marriage License

As our government and society remove a Holy God from public life, Bible-believing Christians can expect more obstacles, trials and difficulties to overcome when dealing with the state. The government is legislating more and more wickedness in opposition to the Living God of heaven and earth. There will be additional challenges for married couples who are Bible believing Christians. Maintaining their marriages, while being yoked to the state, in this three party contract is an unnecessary burden. No married couple desires divorce. As the government redefines marriage terms and conditions, there will be a direct affect on Christian heterosexual marriages. All of this takes place in the spiritual realm first and then in the physical realm. The state redefining the idea of marriage directly affects all current marriages through the contracted body of law – marriage license covenant.

We know Jesus and Paul advise the single life (abstaining from any sexual relations - living a life of purity). This is preferred over the troubles or trials of the married life. The "voluntary" state marriage license adds additional weight and burden to the marriage relationship.

The power of "agreement" in the spiritual realm is everything. The demonic can influence any believer in Jesus Christ, just as easily as a non-believer. Bondage comes about through agreement in any form with the demonic realm. There are three forms of agreement – they come in words spoken, thoughts believed, or words written.

Participating in inner healing ministry for over ten years, I have seen first hand what the power of agreement does to keep an individual in bondage. It is only when the individual comes out of agreement with a particular lie, does their freedom come forth. One example comes to mind. A girl came to receive ministry, repeatedly, for depression. Nobody knew how to address this problem. When she finally asked the Holy Spirit where the lie came in, she was able to get free. Apparently, her uncle said something to her at the age of ten and she agreed with it. She agreed with the lie at a young age. The girl renounced the lie and the depression lifted instantly. She left with a smile on her face. We never saw her again, praise Jesus!

Similarly, the state license agreement affects our marriages adversely, because of the immoral statutes and law legislated. While people can still function agreeing with a certain lie, marriages too can still function, agreeing with the state. The point is, God has more for us and we can experience greater freedoms, tangible and intangible without such agreements.

23 And the word of the LORD came to me, saying, 24 "Son of man, say to her: 'You [are] a land that is not cleansed or rained on in the day of indignation.'

25 "The conspiracy of her prophets in her midst is like a roaring lion tearing the prey; they have devoured people; they have taken treasure and precious things; they have made many widows in her midst.

26 "Her priests have violated My law and profaned My holy things; they have not distinguished between the holy and unholy, nor have they made known [the difference] between the unclean and the clean; and they have hidden their eyes from My Sabbaths, so that I am profaned among them. (Ezekiel 22:23-26 NKJV)

Let us distinguish between the holy and unholy, the clean and unclean.

No Condemnation

1 [There is] therefore now no condemnation to those who are in Christ Jesus, who do not walk according to the flesh, but according to the Spirit. (Romans 8:1 NKJV)

A Word from James

Scripture from James chapter 4:

Adulterers and [fn] adulteresses! Do you not know that friendship with the world is enmity with God? Whoever therefore wants to be a friend of the world makes himself an enemy of God. Or do you think that the Scripture says in vain, "The Spirit who dwells in us yearns jealously"?

But He gives more grace. Therefore He says: "God resists the proud, But gives grace to the humble." Therefore submit to God. Resist the devil and he will flee from you. Draw near to God and He will draw near to you. Cleanse [your] hands, [you] sinners; and purify [your] hearts, [you] double-minded.

Lament and mourn and weep! Let your laughter be turned to mourning and [your] joy to gloom. Humble yourselves in the sight of the Lord, and He will lift you up. (James 4:4-10 NKJV)

The book of James is packed with so much intense goodness. He gets right to the point. James 4:4, hits it on the head. Our nation is filled with adultery; in and out of the Church. The physical reality of adultery taking place in this country, is a parallel to what is taking place in the spiritual realm as well. The Church has become friends with the world. There are too many agreements with this world system. What does adultery in our relationship with the Living God look like? Seeking the face of God individually and collectively as His people, will begin to reveal the truth.

The Holy Spirit wants us. We compromise by embracing the world system over the King of Heaven. God is jealous for us as individuals, families, communities, and nations. He exhorts us to not have any idols or make graven images on earth, heaven or sea below.

4 "You shall not make for yourself a carved image--any likeness [of anything] that [is] in heaven above, or that [is] in the earth beneath, or that [is] in the water under the earth; 5 you shall not bow down to them nor serve them. For I, the LORD your God, [am] a jealous God, visiting the iniquity of the fathers upon the children to the third and fourth [generations] of those who hate Me, 6 but showing mercy to thousands, to those who love Me and keep My commandments. (Exodus 20:4-6 NKJV)

Anything put before God is considered an idol. Replenish your soul in Him. The Word of God is a lamp unto our feet and the law is the path. Psalm 119.

James continues to expound upon the goodness of God, "He gives more grace." We commit adultery with God in the way we love the things of this world. He extends even more grace when we do. He is so good! Worthy is the Lamb that was slain! Next, we see how James says to respond. In one word, "REPENT." In other words "change your mind." We are a double minded and prideful people. We need to cleanse our hearts and hands. The Word of God needs to be our perspective, not our perspective interpreting the Word of God.

Prayer

Father in Heaven, I thank You that You hear our prayers. Thank You for Your amazing grace! Thank You for helping us by the power of Your Holy Spirit, to return to our first love - You. Help us to walk faithfully, rightly dividing the Word of God with truth and righteousness. Help us to discern the clean from the unclean. Help us to walk humbly, love mercy and do justly in all our being. Let wisdom come upon Your marriages. Let wisdom come upon singles considering marriage. Let hunger for Your perfect will come forth in might and power in profound measure like the world has never seen. Let wisdom and discernment come forth for those seeking dissolution from the state. Bring all the questions and answers each couple needs to address, their marriage relationship rightly. I ask that You surround these couples with righteous counsel. I ask for Your warring and ministering angels to encamp about Your people prayerfully considering what to do with this information. Place a fiery hedge of protection around them. Thank You for endowing Your Church in humility, meekness and faithfulness in the days coming forth. Heal marriages Lord, every broken marriage that needs Your touch. I ask for great grace and rich mercy to pour out on all families in the earth right now. Do a radical work of transformation in the hearts of man, to love You first and then love our neighbor as our self. Come Holy Spirit and breathe afresh on Your people. In Y'shua's mighty name. Amen. Thank You.

10

ADULTERY, DIVORCE & VOWS

Some people might make the argument common law marriage is used when two people are not sincere in their commitment to each other. Frankly, for followers of Jesus, nothing could be further from the truth. Marriage is a very real and holy commitment. Professing believers need to grasp the depths of the marriage commitment. We will take a more intimate look at the Word of God and gain Jesus' perspective surrounding the marriage covenant.

What are we aiming for? Please take a moment to read this short, yet powerful Psalm of David. Take a moment to meditate and dialogue with the Holy Spirit on Psalm 15 right now, if you are able. The Psalm is rich with virtue.

Psalm 15

1 A psalm of David. LORD, who may dwell in your sacred tent? Who may live on your holy mountain?

2 The one whose walk is blameless, who does what is righteous, who speaks the truth from their heart; 3 whose tongue utters no slander, who does no wrong to a neighbor, and casts no slur on others;

4 who despises a vile person but honors those who fear the LORD; who keeps an oath even when it hurts, and does not change their mind;

5 who lends money to the poor without interest; who does not accept a bribe against the innocent. Whoever does these things will never be shaken. (Psalm 15:1-5 NIV)

This Psalm is an amazing invitation from the Lord. The psalmist lays out the characteristics of what it takes to dwell in God's sacred tent and live on God's holy mountain. Focusing on verse 4 is the important idea to keep in mind for this chapter. Are we a people who will "keep our oath/s even when it hurts, and not change our mind?" What if we could truly tap into the fear of the LORD? Keeping our oaths, vows and promises will become more possible, "even easier perhaps?" Jesus brings clarification to oaths in Matthew 5:

"Again, you have heard that it was said to the people long ago, 'Do not break your oath, but fulfill to the Lord the vows you have made.' 34 But I tell you, do not swear an oath at all: either by heaven, for it is God's throne; 35 or by the earth, for it is his footstool; or by Jerusalem, for it is the city of the Great King. 36 And do not swear by your head, for you cannot make even one hair white or black. 37 All you need to say is simply 'Yes' or 'No'; anything beyond this comes from the evil one. (*Matthew 5:33-37*)

Highlighting three points in Jesus' statement above:

1. Generally when we attend a wedding, we hear vows recited by the bride and groom. Though they speak to one another, the vows are to be fulfilled unto the LORD, more so than to your spouse. It appears as though the vows are to be kept towards the man and woman. the man and woman made to e. Jesus is communicating in this passage the vows are really being spoken to the LORD. Our marital vows are to be fulfilled unto Him, more so than to . In keeping our wedding vows, we express love to God and then love to our neighbor – your husband or wife to be.

2. Simply let your yes be yes and your no be no. Do your best to make commitments you aim to keep.

3. Going beyond, “yes and no” is from the evil one. Clearly we want to avoid ensnaring ourselves unnecessarily or in a harmful capacity.

Approaching Marriage from God's Word for Two Believers in Jesus

For the purposes of this chapter let us focus the conversation at followers of Jesus who desire to approach marriage from God's perspective, will and purposes. These individuals would confess, "Jesus is my LORD, Master and Savior." This would include, people who are looking to enter holy matrimony for the first time or have been widowed.

Secondarily, this chapter might be of interest to those who are married, have been married, divorced, remarried and those considering remarriage. For this audience, interpreting Scripture accurately for their personal situation, will need to be addressed, by the individual on a case-by-case and situation-by-situation basis. Understanding the topic of divorce and remarriage, deserves the utmost respect and consideration as to how to live righteously in the sight of Jesus Christ. This chapter is not focused at unbelievers or relationships where one is a believer and the other is not.

To gain full understanding of marriage, we need to bring up the topics of adultery, divorce and remarriage from a biblical perspective. Let us dialogue on the topics of adultery, divorce and keeping vows. God is quite serious about this commitment, because the consequences down the road are substantial. Wise decisions help prevent experiencing pain and death. Thankfully, regardless of good or bad decisions, there is mercy, grace and love offered to overcome any situation, through the power of the Holy Spirit and the name of Jesus Christ.

Humanity does not nearly value nor respect marriage as intensely as God. We need to understand, with or without the marriage license, the purpose of marriage is to stay together until the end. It is not recommended anyone should go into marriage with one foot in and the other foot out. Wavering as to whether or not one intends to stay committed, pure and faithful is what Jesus would call "foolish," according to Matthew 7:26. This is written in the context of the Sermon on the Mount – Matthew 5-7.

Jesus raises the standard in Matthew 5 and calls His Church to operate from a higher place because they are now empowered by the Holy Spirit. Through the death of Jesus on the cross and His resurrection, the baptism of the Holy Spirit empowers God's people with the grace to walk as Jesus walked. The same Spirit that raised Jesus from the dead, is now in the born again baptized believer in Jesus. With that being said, keep in mind love is sacrificial – which means giving something up for another. It is not an emotional infatuation that feels good for a moment and when the moment's over, you walk away from the marriage. That is selfish and narcissistic, the opposite of love.

In God's eyes, there is a call to "die" in every way to your single life, once united with your spouse. Jesus says, "It's because of your hardness of heart that Moses permitted a certificate of divorce, but in the beginning it was not so."

Let us explore three topics interconnected to marriage: adultery, divorce and remarriage. Marriage is the biggest commitment made to another human. The purpose for this exploration is to fully capture God's heart for the respect and appreciation He has for the covenant relationship between husband and wife.

Adultery

Let us develop a grid or viewpoint from what some of the Scriptures say regarding "adultery."

- *14 "You shall not commit adultery. (Exodus 20:14 NKJV)*
- *10 'The man who commits adultery with [another] man's wife, [he] who commits adultery with his neighbor's wife, the*

adulterer and the adulteress, shall surely be put to death. (Leviticus 20:10 NKJV)

- *18 'You shall not commit adultery. (Deuteronomy 5:18 NKJV)*
- *32 Whoever commits adultery with a woman lacks understanding; He [who] does so destroys his own soul. (Proverbs 6:32 NKJV)*
- *All of Jeremiah 3 – you will need to look this one up.*
- *14 Also I have seen a horrible thing in the prophets of Jerusalem: They commit adultery and walk in lies; They also strengthen the hands of evildoers, So that no one turns back from his wickedness. All of them are like Sodom to Me, And her inhabitants like Gomorrah. 15 "Therefore thus says the LORD of hosts concerning the prophets: 'Behold, I will feed them with wormwood, And make them drink the water of gall; For from the prophets of Jerusalem Profaneness has gone out into all the land.' " (Jeremiah 23:14-15 NKJV)*
- *37 "For they have committed adultery, and blood [is] on their hands. They have committed adultery with their idols, and even [sacrificed] their sons whom they bore to Me, passing them through [the fire], to devour [them]. (Ezekiel 23:37 NKJV)*
- *All of Hosea 4 – you will need to look this one up.*
- *27 "You have heard that it was said to those of old, 'You shall not commit adultery.' 28 "But I say to you that whoever looks at a woman to lust for her has already committed adultery with her in his heart. 29 "If your right eye causes you to sin, pluck it out and cast [it] from you; for it is more profitable for you that one of your members perish, than for your whole body to be cast into hell. 30 "And if your right*

hand causes you to sin, cut it off and cast [it] from you; for it is more profitable for you that one of your members perish, than for your whole body to be cast into hell. (Matthew 5:27-30 NKJV)

- *20 "Nevertheless I have a few things against you, because you allow that woman Jezebel, who calls herself a prophetess, to teach and seduce My servants to commit sexual immorality and eat things sacrificed to idols. 21 "And I gave her time to repent of her sexual immorality, and she did not repent. 22 "Indeed I will cast her into a sickbed, and those who commit adultery with her into great tribulation, unless they repent of their deeds. 23 "I will kill her children with death, and all the churches shall know that I am He who searches the minds and hearts. And I will give to each one of you according to your works. (Revelation 2:20-23 NKJV)*

Recapping the previous scripture references, we can glean more understanding as to God's feelings regarding the sin of adultery. Here are several points:

1. Commanded: Do not commit adultery.

2. If an individual commits adultery they are instantly put to death under the old covenant.

3. If an individual commits adultery they lack understanding and destroy their own soul.

4. Adulterer's likened to Sodom and Gomorrah, eat wormwood, drink gall and profaneness has gone

out into all the land.

5. Pagans do such practices.

6. Jesus raises the standard and makes adultery an issue of the heart, not just the outward act. Looking with lust, the consequence is being in danger of being cast into hell.

7. Jesus will throw Jezebel on a sickbed. Those who commit adultery with Jezebel will go into the great tribulation, unless they repent. Jesus will kill her children.

The God of the Bible, Jesus Christ is quite serious about the issue of adultery because it is so harmful to the individual. The fruit of adultery causes separation between husband and wife and also separation from God.

God deeply loves people. He is the Good Shepherd who wants to protect His sheep. He is communicating the extreme danger for those who participate in the sin of adultery. For individuals who believe and make the confession that Jesus is their LORD, Savior and Master, are poorly served to dismiss the sin of adultery as a trite thing. This is a very big deal to the heart of God. Jesus will judge all sin with perfect justice. Thankfully, for believers, we are under the blood and our sins are paid for by the finished work of the cross.

Looking with Lust

If your right eye causes you to sin, pluck it out and cast [it] from you; for it is more profitable for you that one of your members perish, than for your whole body to be cast into hell. (Matthew 5:29)

According to Jesus, if we look at an individual with lust in our eyes we have already committed adultery. We are in danger of eternal separation from God! Watching pornography is lusting, thereby committing adultery, subjecting the individual to the real possibility of being cast directly into hell! Hell! The Lake of Fire! How much worse is hell than simply dying, as was the punishment in the Old Covenant? We need to let this perspective sink in, meditate on Jesus' words on the subject matter.

He also warns:

28 "And do not fear those who kill the body but cannot kill the soul. But rather fear Him who is able to destroy both soul and body in hell. (Matthew 10:28 NKJV)

Let us stop justifying our actions and will, in place of God's

Word and Spirit.

I am tremendously convicted right now and sense the weighty "fear of the LORD" over this subject. This is a major problem and issue of concern. Let us not gloss over the warnings and exhortation of Jesus in this conversation. The Author of Life, warning us of His judgment, and ultimately hell fire.

Who, but Jesus really knows how great His mercy is? How great is His grace? How narrow is the narrow path? How few are the few who find it? These are some difficult questions.

A Word from James and Paul

Adulterers and adulteresses! Do you not know that friendship with the world is enmity with God? Whoever therefore wants to be a friend of the world makes himself an enemy of God. 5 Or do you think that the Scripture says in vain, "The Spirit who dwells in us yearns jealously"? 6 But He gives more grace. Therefore He says: "God resists the proud, But gives grace to the humble." (James 4:4-6 NKJV)

"I say then: Walk in the Spirit, and you shall not fulfill the lust of the flesh." (Galatians 5:16 NKJV)

His Word is sure and true. Why would we not want to press into fullness of purity? The Holy Spirit is our helper, to no longer participate in such practices. Holy Spirit's presence, empowers us to overcome the things of the flesh. For the believer, we rejoice in the mercy and grace of Jesus and for our name being written in the Lamb's Book of Life. Yet, we know participating in sin will reap death, in some form, for believer and unbeliever alike. We want to avoid such pain and this is what we are addressing.

23 For the wages of sin [is] death, but the gift of God [is] eternal life in Christ Jesus our Lord. (Romans 6:23 NKJV)

Prayer

Father in Heaven, I repent for all the ways in which I have been guilty of committing adultery in my heart. Bring Your light to the areas of my heart needing Your change. Have mercy on me LORD. Thank You for forgiving me. Have mercy on us as a people and grant us the gift of true repentance. Holy Spirit I invite Your truth to come and change me. I lift up the inhabitants of the earth, LORD, I ask that You cast down the adulterous, lustful spirit. Let all people turn from this wickedness and unrighteousness. Let there be a return to righteousness and purity. Moreover, let Your children love purity and seek righteousness in great measure. Let Your people walk with hearts after You, hating unrighteousness. In the mighty name of Jesus Christ of Nazareth. Amen. Thank You LORD.

In closing out the topic of adultery, let us look at one last scripture discussing this topic.

Stoning the Woman in Adultery

3 Then the scribes and Pharisees brought to Him a woman caught in
adultery. And when they had set her in the midst, 4 they said to
Him, "Teacher, this woman was caught in adultery, in the very act. 5
"Now Moses, in the law, commanded us that such should be stoned.
But what do You say?" 6 This they said, testing Him, that they
might have [something] of which to accuse Him. But Jesus stooped
down and wrote on the ground with [His] finger, as though He did
not hear. 7 So when they continued asking Him, He raised Himself
up and said to them, "He who is without sin among you, let him
throw a stone at her first." 8 And again He stooped down and wrote
on the ground. 9 Then those who heard [it], being convicted by [their]
conscience, went out one by one, beginning with the oldest [even] to the
last. And Jesus was left alone, and the woman standing in the midst.
10 When Jesus had raised Himself up and saw no one but the
woman, He said to her, "Woman, where are those accusers of yours?
Has no one condemned you?" 11 She said, "No one, Lord." And
Jesus said to her, "Neither do I condemn you; go and sin no more."
(John 8:3-11 NKJV)

- Where is the man who was caught in adultery? It takes two to commit adultery (from a physical standpoint), so whom were the Pharisees failing to bring accusation upon? There is already a level of hypocrisy taking place on behalf of the Pharisees by leaving out the other party to the crime.

- Their test was flawed. Jesus knew this full-well. A true test would bring both adulterer and adulteress forward, according to the law and Scripture in Leviticus 20:10.

- Their own sin is exposed. The deceitfulness of their hypocrisy is revealed in their protection of the male. Both male and female should have become subject to the judgment of stoning. The Pharisees showed mercy and grace to the man by not exposing him, but condemnation to the woman.

- What was Jesus writing in the dirt? There is much speculation as to what He was writing. One idea is that He was writing the ten commandments or Scripture like Leviticus 20:10. Reminding the hypocrites that they too are sinners, along with the man they failed to put on trial.

- Jesus demonstrated compassion, mercy and grace towards this adulterous woman.

He protected her from the fullness of the law, as the Pharisees protected their colleague, friend or relative from the fullness of the law.

- Jesus fully hates sin, yet fully loves people. He is zealous for humanity. He wants people to experience the abundant life. There are significant consequences when we take part in any kind of sin, adultery included. When Jesus says, "...go and sin no more" I believe this woman repented and never committed the sin of adultery again. Being in a life and death situation because of her previous actions, she was forgiven much. While today we do not stone people for committing adultery, the cost is potentially greater. The implications affect one's soul and emotions. The pain and suffering do not go away with time. Living with this trauma, over a lifetime, could potentially be a worse punishment than being stoned immediately. We, as a people, need a healthy dose of the fear of the LORD, while receiving His tremendous mercy and grace. All we need to do is confess our sins. He is faithful and just to forgive us and wash away the condemnation and shame.

Jesus demonstrates mercy and grace, not only for the adulterous woman, but also for all the people who were around Him. He could have risen up and judged all the people perfectly. Jesus exemplified compassion on all those who were present in this setting. He knew all of their sins and condemned no one directly.

He came as a Lamb the first time. He is coming as a Lion next time. Jesus will bring justice upon all wickedness and will judge it all righteously.

When Two Believers Divorce

31 "Furthermore it has been said, 'Whoever divorces his wife, let him give her a certificate of divorce.' 32 "But I say to you that whoever divorces his wife for any reason except sexual immorality causes her to commit adultery; and whoever marries a woman who is divorced commits adultery. (Matthew 5:31-32 NKJV)

- If she commits sexual immorality, then she is already an adulteress, yes? Regardless it seems divorce makes the divorcee an adulteress regardless.

- Divorcing a wife for any reason outside of sexual immorality causes her to commit adultery. Anyone who marries the divorced woman commits adultery as well.

3 The Pharisees also came to Him, testing Him, and saying to Him, "Is it lawful for a man to divorce his wife for [just] any reason?" 4 And He answered and said to them, "Have you not read that He who made [them] at the beginning 'made them male and female,' 5 "and said, 'For this reason a man shall leave his father and mother and be joined to his wife, and the two shall become one flesh'? 6 "So then, they are no longer two but one flesh. Therefore what God has joined together, let not man separate." 7 They said to Him, "Why then did Moses command to give a certificate of divorce, and to put her away?" 8 He said to them, "Moses, because of the hardness of your hearts, permitted you to divorce your wives, but from the beginning it was not so. 9 "And I say to you, whoever divorces his wife, except for sexual immorality, and marries another, commits adultery; and whoever marries her who is divorced commits adultery." 10 His disciples said to Him, "If such is the case of the man with [his] wife, it is better not to marry." (Matthew 19:3-10 NKJV)

- In verse 6, Jesus says when two come together in marriage, let no man separate. The understanding here, is that under no circumstance, may anyone separate a couple.

- The Pharisees understood what He was saying, which went against the idea of a "man" issuing a certificate of divorce, which would be a separation, going against Jesus' words in verse 6. They bring up the question about Moses in verse 7. It is the hardness of heart, a lack of love that allowed for a divorce certificate to be issued.

- Notice verse 9, if a man divorces his wife (for any other reason besides sexual immorality) and re-marries another woman, he commits adultery. Agree or not, I read this as, "if a man divorces a woman for any reason other than sexual immorality and gets re-married he is committing "on-going adultery."

Jesus points out in the book of Mark this issue of adultery is a two-way street. Men are just as guilty as women. There is no double-standard in His eyes.

11 So He said to them, "Whoever divorces his wife and marries another commits adultery against her. 12 "And if a woman divorces her husband and marries another, she commits adultery." (Mark 10:11-12 NKJV)

Adultery by definition is having sex with someone other than their spouse. Look up the definition for yourself. Jesus is saying, this form of "remarriage," is simply defined as adultery, not something sanctified with His blessing. He is communicating for the married couple that divorces, remarriage is adultery. Any marital or sexual relationship after divorce, is invalid. The two options for the original couple is reconcile or celibacy. The original marriage covenant is what Jesus identifies as holy matrimony and sanctified in His eyes. He does not validate this second marriage in any capacity throughout scripture. He only identifies it as adultery.

Clarifying the matter at hand, the man marrying the divorced woman, he commits "on-going adultery." If the original couple divorces and both remarry, there are a total of four people committing on-going adultery.

Here is why the term, "on-going adultery" is used. Jesus calls the spouse that re-marries an adulterer. When does adultery come into the equation? When the two become married. What happens when two people marry? They have sex. Jesus calls this adultery. Does that mean the first time they have sex is adultery and thereafter it is no longer adultery? Why would it? If it were adultery the first time the couple has sex, wouldn't the case be true for the 50th, 100th, 1000th time etc.? Jesus never indicates a timetable for when the adultery ends. He simply communicates that the two in question - commit adultery.

3 Options for Two Believers Regarding Divorce

There are three options for a man or woman who divorces, for any reason:

1. Divorce, never get married again and live a life of celibacy.

2. Wait until the divorced spouse dies. Death is the only thing that breaks the covenant of marriage in God's eyes. Once this occurs, the remaining spouse is free to remarry.

3. The previously married couple change their mind about the divorce and reconcile. They humble themselves before God and their spouse, reconcile and unite again.

Sadly, culture and Hollywood's message have completely

destroyed the sacred and holy dynamic God intended for marriage. Commonly, we see couples marry, live together for a bit of time and when they are not happy or personally gratified in some regard – they walk away. How often do we see movie stars setting an example of marrying 2, 3, 4, 5 times, not to mention all the sexual immorality coinciding with the turn-over? We begin to believe and accept this lie as normal life, as if it is okay to join in with this depravity. People who claim to be followers of Jesus, are to rise to the standard of Jesus Christ Himself, in the power of the Holy Spirit. We have the grace to rise up, because God has poured out His Spirit upon us.

Generally speaking the Church, has room to grow in keeping their commitments and word. All too often we act double-minded. The time is now to confess sin and "change our mind" according to righteousness stated in the Bible. What if the Church could stop doing what is right in its own eyes? Love and marriage are not always easy. Marriage requires two people focused on Jesus. Couples need integrity, character, and sacrificial love in order to make it to the end - faithful, holy and pure. Leaning into God and His Word is what makes that possible.

Vows

33 "Again you have heard that it was said to those of old, 'You shall not swear falsely, but <u>*shall perform your oaths to the Lord.*</u>*' 34 "But I say to you, do not swear at all: neither by heaven, for it is God's throne; 35 "nor by the earth, for it is His footstool; nor by Jerusalem, for it is the city of the great King. 36 "Nor shall you swear by your head, because you cannot make one hair white or black. 37 "But let your 'Yes' be 'Yes,' and your 'No,' 'No.' For whatever is more than these is from the evil one. (Matthew 5:33-37 NKJV)*

Notice in verse 33 how Jesus instructs us to, "perform your oaths to the Lord." During a wedding, generally the bride and groom communicate vows to one another. Jesus is saying, these vows are to be performed to the Lord, rather than to the spouse as the case might be. Fulfilling our vows or oaths to the Lord by default will include fulfilling our vows to our spouse. When the rubber meets the road as the case might be, our commitment is to the Lord more so than to our spouse. In a sense, in breaking our commitment we are first letting the Lord and then our spouse down.

If we make a marital commitment to an individual, the righteous thing to do is stick it out, no matter how challenging or bad it seems. For two self-proclaimed followers of Jesus, walking away from the marriage outside of sexual immorality is sin. Even then, divorce is not Jesus' heart for marriage. His desire is for the couple to remain together. Keep in mind, separation may be a necessary option for a season of time. One spouse may need to deal with issues that make it unsafe for the other spouse to live under the same roof. This is not divorce, but simply waiting upon the LORD to bring salvation to an area the enemy has attacked and wounded the other spouse.

We have no one to blame for our spousal decision. If we made a poor choice, that is our responsibility. Nobody holds a gun to our head forcing us to marry. Standing before the Most High God and a group of people, committing devotion to another for the rest of our life, is something we need to follow through on. Running away from our commitment is not the answer. We cannot say, "Oops I made a mistake. I did not realize all of these other things needed to be considered first." Sadly, it is really too late after the fact. There is no turning back. The good news is, nothing is too far-gone for the healing touch and deliverance of the Most High God. He makes all things beautiful in its time.

Psalm 15 talks about fulfilling our obligations, even at one's own expense. Divorce is shortsighted this side of eternity. Keeping our eyes on eternity, makes the follow-through on marriage, worthwhile. Gary Thomas' book "Sacred Marriage" is a great read that develops this idea of keeping eternity in mind through your marriage. I highly recommend this book which expounds upon the true nature of marriage, not Hollywood's depiction. One example he uses in the book is that of Abraham Lincoln. He was arguably the best President this nation has ever seen, while his wife was arguably the worst first lady. Gary tells the story of how Abraham's marriage and wife were used to fortify his character to withstand the challenges of his call as President of the United states of America. Gary's perspective of God's purpose for marriage is both sobering and inspiring.

The only thing divorce proves is how weak our love is and our faithlessness to believe God's Word. We must believe Jesus is capable of working things out, "for the good of those who are called according to His purposes."

Jesus has much to say about adultery, divorce and keeping our vows. In fact, they go hand in hand when He speaks about it in Matthew 5. The entire chapter is applicable to the marriage relationship. After investigating these ideas it is clear marriage requires an intense level of commitment by a people of character, integrity and virtue.

Prayer

Father God, thank You for Your Word of truth. Let us become a people after Your heart, after Your Word and led by Your Holy Spirit. Help us to be single-minded, to count the cost and to persevere to the end. Let us be a people of self-control. Thank You that Your Holy Spirit empowers us to walk as Jesus walked, rising to His standard. Thank You that Jesus is worth the reward of His suffering. Help us to take up our cross and follow Your example Jesus. Let Your light come forth in great power. Thank You that Your love covers a multitude of sins. We love You Jesus, in Your name. Amen.

To Those Divorced and Possibly Remarried

This chapter is directed at those believers in Jesus, who are single, have never been married or widowed, and considering marriage. Should the individual decide to marry without a marriage license, the Bible and Jesus clearly articulate the intensity of the marriage covenant. This relationship is not to be taken lightly. As some might make claim, the reason for desiring common law marriage is because "You are not really committed" or some other weak argument. According to God's Word, that could not be further from the truth.

If you are reading this book and have been married before, desire to remarry or are already remarried, seek the Lord's answer in His Word. For the purposes of the book, we will not be exploring "all" the possible scenarios of remarriage, nor defining anything beyond what has been stated. Some scenarios might include and are not limited to:

1. You were both unbelievers when you married.

2. Your spouse lied to you. They were not a believer in Jesus.

3. Adultery took place.

The list could go on.

The Words of Jesus are real, gracious and filled with truth. How are we going to walk this out in light of His Words? If we love Him, we obey His commands. The wages of sin is death. Any time people, saved or unsaved, participate in sin, the promise of death exists in one form or another. Let the Holy Spirit speak to you through the Words of Jesus. His conviction and truth are gracious and right. Everyone will stand before the perfect One, individually for his or her actions. One Man's thoughts are all that matter on the Day of Judgment. How we choose to walk our lives out now, will affect us for all eternity. We only get one shot at this thing called life. There are no second chances, once our flesh falls limp.

Lastly, all of humanity falls short of the glory of God. The beauty of the Cross of Calvary is for those who confess Jesus Christ as LORD and Savior. The blood of Jesus covers *all* of our sin. The awesome reality of being a Christian is the complete recognition of our desperation for a Savior in Christ Jesus. Let us not continue in our sins, but respect the blood shed for us to defeat sin and death in our lives, through true repentance. Obeying Jesus' commands is our evidence of love towards Him. Love Him. Love Him well. He is worthy!

Major Update as of 07.23.2022

My publication of this book and sale of copies does not mean I have exhausted my exploration or learning about marriage from the perspective of the Bible. In regards to the original Greek text, I have learned something new. I'm not sure how you felt about the previous elements of this chapter? Based on translation, that entire perspective seems to be in question.

Apparently, the word that we see in Matthew (NKJV) and the new testament in the Bible that says "divorce" in the Greek actually is interpreted, "put away." The question is, what does "put away" mean and is it the same as divorce or not? [26]

Check out BlueLetterBible.org or a concordance and see for yourself. When looking at the Greek where divorce is used in our Bibles, the translation is actually "shall put away," not divorce. There is a substantial difference between "put away" and the word "divorce." You can see one example in Matthew 5:31.

g630: ἀπολύω *apolyō* – shall put away

[26] http://www.christianpoly.org/divorce.php

We know that in the old testament there was room for divorce. So did Jesus change things up or did He stay consistent with the law of Moses?

1 "When a man takes a wife and marries her, and it happens that she finds no favor in his eyes because he has found some uncleanness in her, and he writes her a certificate of divorce, puts it in her hand, and sends her out of his house, 2 "when she has departed from his house, and goes and becomes another man's wife, 3 "if the latter husband detests her and writes her a certificate of divorce, puts it in her hand, and sends her out of his house, or if the latter husband dies who took her as his wife, 4 "then her former husband who divorced her must not take her back to be his wife after she has been defiled; for that is an abomination before the LORD, and you shall not bring sin on the land which the LORD your God is giving you as an inheritance. - Deuteronomy 24:1-4 NKJV

The law of God through Moses permitted the idea of divorce. Then Jesus came along and gave the sermon on the mount, plus other teachings on the reality of marriage. He seemed to raise the standard in several ways and when reading Bible translations today, at first glance it would appear that was the case for marriage, divorce and remarriage.

Our translations use the word "divorce." In the Greek the translation is "put away" or "send away." Today, "put away" would be equivalent to "separated." There is a significant difference in these two ideas. Of course, if a couple is "separated" and not legally divorced, then marrying someone else who is "separated" would be adultery. When a man divorced a woman, he was to give her the dowry back and to officially divorce her. He wasn't required to return the dowry if he didn't divorce her. It was evil or greedy behavior on the part of the men, as they did not give back the dowry and didn't divorce the woman properly, but instead were just separating from her. As a separated woman, the woman would clearly be guilty of adultery if she got into relationships with anyone.

What needed to take place in the old and new testament were to separate AND give a certificate of divorce (lawfully divorce). It may seem as though Jesus was speaking to those who were separated and not actually lawfully divorced.

The word divorce is used in the old testament as follows:

Deuteronomy 24:1, 24:3, Isaiah 50:1, Jeremiah 3:8 – in the Hebrew text. Strong's Concordance H3748 -
kᵊrîṯûṯ pronounced ker-ee-thooth'

It would seem that the Greek word, apoluo "put away" and in Hebrew Shalach H7971 "cast away or send away" is not the same as divorce.

Divorce and send away are two different ideas, purposes and meanings.

Here are a couple more website pages you might find helpful to look at for yourself along with the Strong's Concordance and an Interlinear Greek and English Bible.

https://www.divorcehope.com/shalachapoluoputtethaway.htm
https://www.divorcehope.com/apoluoshalachputtethaway.htm

Make no mistake, the Lord hates divorce. This update is not to advocate divorce in any capacity. The point that I'm hoping to convey is it would appear that divorce was permitted in the new testament when done lawfully, that remarriage is permitted and isn't considered adultery (like it would seem if we simply read our Bible at face value) without exploring the Greek translation first.

Divorce, remarriage, and marriage are delicate subjects that require each individual to do their own research. We must keep our commitments and believe the Lord is big enough to overcome any obstacles. Please don't take my advice on how to do marriage just because I've put this book together. You need to do the research, pray, think for yourself and come to your own conclusions for your life. I'm doing my best to discern the truth just like you are. Ultimately, we all stand before Jesus alone for our words and actions. The more we take actions in alignment with His word, the better off we will be moving forward into all eternity. This is my aim and goal, to make the best decisions possible moving from this point into eternity with Christ Jesus. I hope all of this helps and encourages you into a closer, deeper relationship with King Jesus.

Lastly, I have learned that we cannot take our translation at face value. In order to ensure that these delicate conversations are translated correctly, it's crucial to look at the original text. Unlike what I thought growing up, I didn't realize we couldn't simply take our Bibles at face value. As I too am a work in progress, I am grateful for your grace and mercy. May God richly bless you.

11

THE HOMOSEXUAL STATE LICENSE

People engaging in homosexual actions are receiving recognized relational status by the dictates of the government. From a biblical perspective, such relationships are not equal or similar to that of heterosexual marriage. "Marriage" is, and always will be, an exclusive relationship defined between one man and one woman, as it has throughout all of human history. There is a battle taking place at the federal and state level right now, over this very issue of homosexual actions becoming lawfully recognized. According to the Bible, the Living God of Abraham, Isaac and Jacob does not acknowledge "homosexual union" in any legal capacity and is simply defined as sin. Scripture does define such activity as "abominable and lawlessness."

The nation's government and the Government of Heaven, do not see eye to eye on this topic. The state and federal government no longer have a clear definition, understanding or appreciation for holy matrimony – one man and one woman.

In a day when marriage and the family unit is under attack from all sides, followers of Jesus Christ need to ask, why? Why are marriages and families in the body of Christ falling apart at unprecedented rates? We know what Karl Marx thinks, "In order to have a perfect socialistic society, you have to destroy the family unit." This is exactly what the government is legislating, condoning and advocating.

Reflect on the simple reality…

- The world government is losing sight of righteousness on all counts, in this case specifically marriage and family.
- Bible believers know homosexual acts have nothing to do with marriage. These acts are unrighteous, unholy and illegal in the sight of a Holy God.
- A "license" is the permission to do something that

would otherwise be illegal.

- It has never been illegal for a man and woman to get married in YHWH's eyes or mankind's eyes for that matter.

The time has come for the people of YHWH to change the way we play the game…

- Stop voluntarily signing the marriage license covenant with the state. Signing this document communicates your belief that for a man and woman to marry, it is a criminal act, that is illegal and requires permission from an unholy governmental system. God called marriage good in His sight.

- If the federal and state government think it is a good idea to license homosexual acts, then by definition, a license is perfectly fitting. Man's wisdom is clearly on display in this conversation and it is a pathetic argument.

Governments condoning sexual perversion of this nature will only invoke the judgment of the Most High God. We know what happened to Sodom and Gomorrah, it was destroyed for sexual perversion. YHWH's people need to separate out from this world governing system.

Bible-believers need to stand against such wicked laws coming to fruition. This is the hour and this is the time we must stand for righteousness. Pray, fast and take action – people's souls and eternal well-being are at stake! With that being said, there are Bible-believing men and women that work within the governmental system. However, the government as a whole, is not submitted to Jesus Christ or the Word of God, and this is the major problem. Pray for the government officials, legislation and for godly men and women to take office. Pray they will not compromise under the pressure of corruption.

Homosexual Acts

Homosexual acts are an abomination before the eyes of the Creator, "illegal" and "unlawful" according to the Word of God. Take a look at the Word of God.

13 'If a man lies with a male as he lies with a woman, both of them have committed an abomination. They shall surely be put to death. Their blood [shall be] upon them. (Leviticus 20:13 NKJV)

Abomination[27]: something abominable: extreme disgust and hatred: loathing.

24 Therefore God also gave them up to uncleanness, in the lusts of their hearts, to dishonor their bodies among themselves, 25 who exchanged the truth of God for the lie, and worshiped and served the

[27] Abomination - By permission. From Merriam-Webster's Collegiate® Dictionary, 11th Edition ©2015 by Merriam-Webster, Inc. (www.Merriam-Webster.com)

creature rather than the Creator, who is blessed forever. Amen.

26 For this reason God gave them up to vile passions. For even their women exchanged the natural use for what is against nature.

27 Likewise also the men, leaving the natural use of the woman, burned in their lust for one another, men with men committing what is shameful, and receiving in themselves the penalty of their error which was due. 28 And even as they did not like to retain God in [their] knowledge, God gave them over to a debased mind, to do those things which are not fitting;

29 being filled with all unrighteousness, sexual immorality, wickedness, covetousness, maliciousness; full of envy, murder, strife, deceit, evil-mindedness; [they are] whisperers, 30 backbiters, haters of God, violent, proud, boasters, inventors of evil things, disobedient to parents, 31 undiscerning, untrustworthy, unloving, unforgiving, unmerciful;

32 who, knowing the righteous judgment of God, that those who practice such things are deserving of death, not only do the same but also approve of those who practice them. (Romans 1:24-32 NKJV)

We are looking at two different government systems. God's Kingdom vs. Satan's Kingdom. Water and oil do not mix. What agreement is there between the righteous and unrighteous?

14 Do not be unequally yoked together with unbelievers. For what fellowship has righteousness with lawlessness? And what communion has light with darkness? (2 Corinthians 6:14 NKJV)

5 You are all sons of light and sons of the day. We are neither of the night nor of darkness. - (1Thessalonians 5:5 NKJV)

9 Do you not know that the unrighteous will not inherit the kingdom of God? Do not be deceived. Neither fornicators, nor idolaters, nor adulterers, nor homosexuals, nor sodomites, 10 nor thieves, nor covetous, nor drunkards, nor revilers, nor extortioners will inherit the kingdom of God. 11 And such were some of you. But you were washed, but you were sanctified, but you were justified in the name of the Lord Jesus and by the Spirit of our God. (1Corinthians 6:9-11 NKJV)

Merriam Webster Changes Definitions

Interesting, Merriam Webster has added to the definition of marriage. They now include the following definition:

Marriage[28]:

... "a similar relationship between people of the same sex"...

..."the state of being united to a person of the same sex in a relationship like that of a traditional marriage"...

---

[28] Marriage - By permission. From Merriam-Webster's Collegiate® Dictionary, 11th Edition ©2015 by Merriam-Webster, Inc. (www.Merriam-Webster.com)

Look up in Merriam Webster the definitions for the words "similar" and "like." Something "similar" will NEVER be "exactly" the same as in this case defined as a relationship between a man and woman in the confines of holy matrimony - marriage. The major reason heterosexual marriages are vastly different from homosexual acts, is due to the physiology and inability to produce offspring. People choosing to engage in homosexual acts do not have the ability to procreate. When a man and man or woman and woman participate solely in homosexual acts, procreation is an impossibility.

The only way procreation would be possible under such a scenario, is if in the depravity and wickedness of man, "modern science" circumvents God's original design. There will never be a baby produced from two homosexual's DNA. Artificial insemination could take place from a male for a female, but that is still not qualified as homosexual procreation.

What if science tampers with humanity? Are we actually attempting to go in a direction allowing a man to become pregnant and a woman altered to produce sperm? Even then, the homosexual relationship would not be justified as marriage in the eyes of the Creator of Heaven and Earth. It would only serve to reveal man's wicked attempt to justify its actions apart from God's original design.

God created man and woman to come together as one flesh. Men and women have distinct traits and qualities. When a man and woman come together, the two become one, where man is weak the woman is stronger and where the woman is weak the man is stronger. Even though dictionary companies are doing their best to associate marriage with people engaging in homosexual acts, the truth is, homosexuals will never fit under the definition of marriage. It would be better for them to create a new term, than poorly attempt to identify its relationship under the umbrella of "marriage." Same-sex relations will always invariably be different from heterosexual marriage relationships. The only thing that is similar is the reality there are two humans, attempting to define a relationship, recognized by law. Outside of that desire, nothing is similar.

Hate Speech

There may be unbelievers (perhaps some professing believers) reading the preceding words and thinking to themselves, "This is hate speech! This guy is ... fill in the blank." I am sorry you might be believing these thoughts and feelings right now. Be assured nothing could be further from the truth. Again, the purpose of this book is to ask the tough questions and uncover the truth, communicating it from a place of love. The truth, in fact, is love. If you happen to be struggling at the moment, please pause. Take a deep breath, take a step back from these emotions and keep reading. Perhaps an in-depth explanation will help bring forth greater understanding of these ideas and thoughts.

The world has become increasingly concerned regarding the "vocabulary or words" used from one human towards another human. The term "politically correct" is basically another name for "word police." It is interesting to point out how the United States of America was actually founded upon the very ability to express "freedom of speech." Some individuals in this country, in recent years, desire and attempt to remove this major founding principle necessary for a "free people" to exist. The supposed "tolerant" preachers have become seemingly the most "intolerant" of words that were written 2000+ years ago. Words in which societies have been formed by and flourished under. Those preaching "tolerance" demonstrate their intolerance when it comes to views opposing sinful lifestyles as communicated from the Bible. Sadly, people want their sin... to their own detriment.

Personally, I hate sin, all sin. Everything God calls sin, I hate, because He hates it and He alone is good. Sin is a *particular action or spoken word* that goes against what God calls good, righteous and just. It is important to point out that people are separate from their actions. People, in and of themselves are not sin. However, humans do things that are considered sinful. Their actions and words, at times are considered sin or sinful.

Sin[29] *a* : an offense against religious or moral lawb : an action that is or is felt to be highly reprehensible <it's a *sin* to waste food>

[29] Sin - By permission. From Merriam-Webster's Collegiate® Dictionary, 11th Edition ©2015 by Merriam-Webster, Inc. (www.Merriam-Webster.com)

c : an often serious shortcoming : fault

2 *a* : *transgression of the law of God* *b* : a vitiated state of human nature in which the self is estranged from God

You might ask, "Why do you hate sin? What is so bad about sin?" Sin causes separation from God, which can lead to death.

The Bible says, "The wages of sin is death." I do not know about you, but personally I do not appreciate death, specifically the death of people around me.

Depending on the closeness and relationship, death can be quite heart breaking. I have lost friends and family to death. I cried much. Physical death of individuals is only one example of the many different kinds of death that can exist. Physical, emotional, spiritual and so on are all examples of different kinds of death that can exist.

Getting back to the topic of the homosexual lifestyle, the Bible is telling the truth, the wages of sin is death. If the entire population became strictly homosexual, the entire human race would become extinct within 100 years, because no reproduction would take place.

Mankind was created specifically for male and female relationships to allow the continuation of humanity from generation to generation.

Practicing homosexuality is a choice, just like heterosexuals having

sex outside the confines of a marriage relationship, identified as fornication. Both forms of sexual immorality are equally detrimental. These actions continually practiced can lead to death.

Again, this is not hate speech towards people or even from God towards mankind. Rather this is actually defining love by providing us with knowledge of right vs. wrong. Believe it or not, God loves mankind. It is true. He loves you. He loves me. He loves all of mankind.

How do I know God loves people?

"For God so loved the world that He gave His only begotten Son, that whoever believes in Him should not perish but have everlasting life." (John 3:16 NKJV)

It is God's desire that none should perish.

He provided the Bible to mankind so as to understand good actions from evil actions. The Bible can be looked at as an instruction manual for life. God's great love for humanity is laid out in this book. In reading the Bible we discover a love story between the Creator and the created. We cannot begin to comprehend His love for us. He loves you so much He gave His Son so that you could be reconciled and restored to relationship with Him. You can talk to Him right now! He is that big. He sees and hears everything you say, do, and think. Be honest with Him. He can handle your honesty. In fact, He values and appreciates honesty.

Jesus laid down His life for sinners while they were still His enemy. I do not know what your current thoughts are regarding Jesus Christ. It is not to late to acknowledge Him as Lord (if you have not already) and make Him Master of your life. He is all-together good. His thoughts for you are like the sands on the seashore, filled with grace, mercy and compassion.

Jesus says, *"Come to Me, all you who labor and are heavy laden, and I will give you rest. 29 "Take My yoke upon you and learn from Me, for I am gentle and lowly in heart, and you will find rest for your souls. 30 "For My yoke [is] easy and My burden is light." (Matthew 11:28-30 NKJV)*

His words are true.

Born Again

Once born again, the believer is instantly translated from being a part of Satan's Kingdom into God's Kingdom. There is a new government by which we operate. We operate under the Lordship of Jesus Christ, His Kingdom, Government and Dominion.

3 Jesus answered and said to him, "Most assuredly, I say to you, unless one is born again, he cannot see the kingdom of God." 4 Nicodemus said to Him, "How can a man be born when he is old? Can he enter a second time into his mother's womb and be born?" 5 Jesus answered, "Most assuredly, I say to you, unless one is born of water and the Spirit, he cannot enter the kingdom of God. (John 3:3-5 NKJV)

9 that if you confess with your mouth the Lord Jesus and believe in your heart that God has raised Him from the dead, you will be saved. 10 For with the heart one believes unto righteousness, and with the mouth confession is made unto salvation. 11 For the Scripture says, "Whoever believes on Him will not be put to shame." ... 13 For "whoever calls on the name of the LORD shall be saved." (Romans 10:9-11, 13 NKJV)

Who Is Legally Married Before God?

According to Bible Scripture who is legally married? A man and woman without a marriage license or two homosexuals with a marriage license?

Why are Christians looking to the state for the validation of their marriage?

As discussed earlier, the government is becoming increasingly muddled on the definition of marriage. God's never been confused over the definition because He defined it. The very idea of marriage came straight from the Creator Himself.

He never communicated, "As long as you get permission from the government, then you can get married." How is it that we have somehow bought into this marriage license lie and come into agreement with it?

You may ask, "But what about the benefits we get from the marriage license?" I say, "Trust God. Trust that the promises in the Scriptures will come true as you follow after Him, being holy set apart. God's benefits will always surpass anything the state could possibly offer you."

On top of trusting God, there is nothing that the state can prohibit you from receiving or accomplishing, with a common law marriage. A common law marriage is just as legal, legitimate and valid – it is simply not "recognized" in some states at this time.

From 5 to 13 to 19 to 37 States with Same Sex Marriage

Initially, when starting this book only five states allowed same sex couples to have a recognized union. In date order, those states are: Massachusetts, Connecticut, Iowa, Vermont and New Hampshire. The District of Columbia also recognized gay marriages as of March 3, 2010. As of April 2015, there were 37 states that permitted homosexual union. The U.S. Supreme Court ruling now allows homosexual union for all 50 states. Who knows what is next? On the basis of "equality" every other type of relationship must be condoned if homosexuals are granted permission to "marry," otherwise it is considered discrimination. We will see incest, pedophilia and beastiality becoming common place because of the ruling

June 26th, 2015.

Why are Christians going to the unrighteous government to have their marriages recognized, something that has been God ordained from the beginning of time?

"When God gave Adam to Eve marriage happened immediately. Without the authority and authorization from God, their marriage would have been wrong. Later, God granted His authority for a couple to marry through His family representative, the Patriarch, or father.

In Scripture, marriage was the uniting of two families in a covenant approved by the fathers, the ecclesiastical authorities, and by God.

The state license leaves divorce as an easy out to a relationship. Thus, we see the bottom line to the license – control and revenue. The license, which cost a few dollars twenty years ago, now costs upwards of fifty dollars. Health Departments are using this revenue to fund projects such as Homes for Unwed Mothers, Homes for Battered Wives, Child Abuse Agencies, and other anti-family and anti-marriage projects. Add to this the divorce costs, which fill the coffers of lawyers, family and juvenile courts, adult and child psychologists, court referees and judges, and many others. The marriage license leads to and fuels an industry that encourages divorce." The Marriage License - Dr. Townsend[30]

The sin of homosexuality is no greater than another sin. All sins are forgivable aside from the blasphemy of the Holy Spirit. Everyone has an opportunity to change their mind, turn towards Jesus and righteousness. Let us give the Word of God its rightful place in our hearts, families and homes. It is time for revival of the Word of God to come upon this land.

[30] http://www.drbentownsend.com/documents/the%20marriage%20license.pdf

12

CHANGING YOUR NAME IS EASY

One of the biggest concerns, in not acquiring a marriage license, is the ability to change one's name. Understandably, married couples want to function under their new relational status. Having a marriage license or not, does not inhibit a married couple from receiving any relational benefit.

I contacted different states as to how one would go about

changing there name and found it took quite some time. After all the research, one lady, in particular, that was actually married without a license, shared the process of how to go about changing your name.

She has a great story, with helpful insight as to how you might go about this for your own marriage.

Trish's Testimony

A Christian woman named Trish and her husbanded had a wedding and opted not to sign the marriage license. Trish explained that up until this point, she only shared this information with a small handful of people. As I understand it, I was only the fourth person she shared with, regarding their lack of a marriage license. This was a Divine appointment. Hearing her story and sharing her testimony with me was a tremendous answer to prayer. Thank You Jesus. I hope her story will offer clarity, in your own journey, as to how you might change your last name.

Leading into marriage, Trish's husband advocated not signing the marriage license. All of this, "no marriage license talk," was new to her. She began to do a thorough investigation of the Scriptures. There was not one example in the Bible indicating she needed a marriage license to be married. Trish simply trusted her husband and God. Upon further prayer and study she realized there was nothing indicating this was a violation of God's will or His Word.

In our conversation, I had other questions for Trish: "Trish, how did you change your name? What about the paperwork with all the different legalities, etc.?" She said, "It was not a problem. Nobody ever asked me to prove our marriage. I simply assumed my husband's last name. When I went to the Social Security department to change the name on my social security card, I simply stated on the application that I got married and filled out the "name change" on my application."

Once she received her updated social security card, changing all other documents was straight forward and without question. She changed her name on her driver's license and bank accounts. They both received health insurance as a married couple. She admitted being nervous throughout this process, however, there were no problems.

Apparently, you do not need to go to a judge to petition the court for a name change. Wow! I am amazed as to how this marriage license is not that big of a deal. People can marry and enjoy life, apart from the influence and involvement of the state. There are so many myths surrounding the state marriage license, it is astounding.

Trish's story does not end there. Unfortunately, her husband filed for divorce in the late 90's. To complete the divorce, they went before the state and filed for divorce within the family court system. *The court viewed their relationship as a marriage, without question.* They divorced, though Trish did not desire this outcome. Nearly 20 years later, she is still contending for restoration and reconciliation, of her marriage and family. She believes that the only option she has is either to remain single or reconcile with her husband. Remarriage is not an option for her, because she believes she is still in a covenant relationship, to the man she married, based upon Jesus' words in Matthew 5. Here is a committed woman of God, that did not need the marriage license to validate her covenant and marriage relationship.

Though Trish's husband is not interested at the moment, I am believing for the Living God to restore this marriage and family. Would you, reader, please lift up a prayer for Trish and her husband right now? Would you contend before the courts of Heaven for the restoration of their marriage and family, regardless of his feelings at the moment?

Father in Heaven, I lift up Trish and her husband right now. I ask that you would restore and reconcile them to each other. I ask that you do a work in both Trish and her husband's life. Let every influencing spirit that is not of You, YHWH, be cast down right now and bound in the Lake of Fire. Thank You for letting Your Holy Spirit come into their lives in those empty places. Fill these vessels and temples for Your glory Jesus, in Your name. Amen.

Changing Your Name - Option #1

For women who want to assume their husbands name after the wedding, simply contact the Social Security department, fill out a name change application, wait for a new card and use that to change your other documents.

Changing Your Name Option #2

Request a court ordered official name change. The following information is based upon the premise that you will need an official court name change and does not take into consideration Trish's testimony.

Arizona: Does Not Recognize Common Law Marriage

I went to the local Arizona Superior Court to find out where and how to change one's name, legally. To my surprise I was directed to the "Law Library." This was my first visit to the "Superior Court."

Once I walked into the "Law Library" an attendant assisted me with a specific type of application needed to apply for a name change. There are different types of applications for a name change based upon your background. In my case, I picked up the application that was for "adult, no minor."

In Arizona, the cost is $311 to change your name (which may have increased by now). The application will actually warn you, that you do not need to file this application if you have gotten married.

"X DO NOT USE THESE FORMS TO CHANGE YOUR NAME BECAUSE YOU GOT

MARRIED.NOTE: You do not need to request a name change through the Court if you get married and want to use your spouse's last name."

This is under the premise you and your spouse signed an Arizona state marriage license. This would not hold true for common law marriage because Arizona does not "recognize" such marriages, though they are legal in all 50 states.

Most state's do not "recognize" common law marriage, changing your name apart from the marriage license will be necessary. You then need a "court petitioned" name change. I recommend coming up with a reason other than, "I got married" for the name change. Most state employees have little knowledge of the details regarding the marriage license. Another reason to petition the court for a name change would be… "I like the sound of Jane Smith better than Jane Doe and I always wanted to change it. I finally got around to it." if this is true for you. Keep in mind that the statement must be true for you. Advocating honesty, integrity and doing things legally is what this book condones. This book points you towards what is legal, as it pertains to marriage. The objective is to legally change your name without involving the state in your marriage.

Keep in mind you probably do not need to go into the Superior Court for the application if you have a printer and internet access. You can print the document up, fill it out, mail it or drop it off to your local Superior Court.

In the state's mind, you are "asking" if it is okay for you to change your name. The state employees I spoke with indicate name changes are commonly permitted.

As a married woman, you can simply communicate with friends, family and colleagues, that you are Mrs. Jane Doe, married to Mr. John Doe. From a legal standpoint, you need a new Social Security card or the court to authorize the name change for "*legal*" purposes. Men could change their names in like fashion if that is of interest.

If I do not have a marriage license, what about changing my name?

The name change does not require a marriage license. Men and women, regularly change their names for a variety of reasons completely unrelated to marriage. Actors are one example of people who change their names because their profession requires it.

I spoke with a friend named Lauren. She lives in Arizona, married using a Hebrew Ketubah or Covenant and refused the marriage license. She appealed to the court for a name change, communicating that she wanted the last name of her "spiritual life partner." The court agreed to this name change. Both Trish and Lauren changed their names in different ways, but the outcome was the same – legal and successful.

Iowa: Recognizes Common Law Marriage

It is challenging to see a difference between states recognizing common law marriage and states that do not.

All states highly advocate the "voluntary" state license, regardless of acknowledging common law or not. In Iowa for example, a marriage license costs $35. You can change your name with the license from the state, rather than paying the $185 for the "petitioned name change." Everyone I spoke with (4 different individuals in different departments - all very wonderful, helpful and friendly) definitely advocated going the "license" route in subtle, yet noticeable ways.

In my discussions there was not much offered in terms of a "how to" program regarding the common law marriage. I spoke with a woman (we will call her "Jane") who legislates the code and law, but she did not know much as to how the code was actually "implemented." She advised I speak with the people who actually implement the code and gave me their phone number.

I followed Jane's advice and discovered it takes about 30 days to change your name with the state of Iowa. The process is as follows:

1. Go to the website for the county clerk

2. Print a copy of the name change application

3. Scan it and email it back to the state, you all get approved with a number to call after 30 days.

4. Then you get an appointment to see the judge. Meet the judge and request name change

Once you are approved, receive certified copies to begin changing your name. Bring your original birth certificate to the state to verify your identity.

I asked if people ever get denied the name change? The lady I spoke with indicated, nobody ever gets denied the name change. In several of the phone calls I was directed to the website www.iowacourts.gov. It was advised to call a family attorney for a consultation and to read the code off the website.

The overwhelming reality of this investigation is… *nobody really knows what is going on within the system.* Everybody referred me to another department because they did not feel they could adequately answer my questions about marriage legalities. I call this "designed ignorance." If no one can answer your questions, then chances are likely, couples will choose the path of least resistance and have no clear understanding. Also, there is a level of fear communicated in the state employees' responses because they do not actually know what to anticipate with the common law marriage option. The marriage license option is clearly mapped out. Common law marriage by nature tends to be a little more ambiguous.

Here are some questions I asked the Iowa employees:

How do you change your last name?

Does the location of the marriage matter?

What are the supposed benefits of having the state recognize your marriage?

Discoveries based upon the Iowa employee's answers:

Nobody gets denied the name petition change in Iowa.

If you get married via common law marriage, you "may" be able to simply assume the last name of the husband. The people I spoke with, again, were not completely certain (further example of designed ignorance mentioned before) and advised speaking with someone else other than them, whether it be another state department or a family attorney. It is advisable to legally change your name to the husband's last name. Having an agreement with a signed affidavit could be enough to get your name changed legally. Speak with a family lawyer from a common law state for advise.

"Jane" (the legislator of code and law referenced earlier), had some interesting viewpoints as to what common law marriage meant to her. In her opinion, couples in common law marriage were not interested in a wedding ceremony. I personally, want everything in terms of a wedding ceremony, a Holy Spirit filled marriage pointing to Jesus Christ, and simply leave out the "voluntary" state marriage license. Such actions would put my marriage in the common law marriage category.

“Jane” also mentioned it would be advisable to have a contract or agreement between you and your spouse. Regarding the location of the wedding, each state has a specific stance as to the importance of location. Iowa, had little concern, other than the couple needed to reside in the state for a period of time.

There is a department specifically designed to handle divorces. This department is totally separate from the department in charge of issuing marriage licenses and certificates. Cindy, from Iowa, indicated she handle's divorces - marriage license or common law marriage divorces. If a common law couple wants to get divorced they come into the court system just as a marriage license couple would. They are then treated the same as couples with a marriage license. Once you subject yourself to their rules, game over. You are now under their jurisdiction.

Hopefully you will be wise enough to put some provisions in place to sort out the unfortunate reality of divorce, should it go that way. Remember, the state wants control and your money. While they do not know anything about successful common law marriages, in terms of keeping records of them on file, they all gladly take part in separating a marriage for any reason.

Kansas: Recognizes Common Law Marriage

Kansas has a form to fill out for couples requesting recognition of their common law marriage. Their form inquires or asks you several questions about the relationship. One very telling question was, "Did you file your last income tax return indicating that you were married?" This is significant because it removes the concern of not being able to file a joint tax return, without a state marriage license. Common law marriages can in fact, file taxes jointly. The fact they ask the question, shows how separate the federal and state government are from one another. This reveals the clear separation of power within the government. *We must be wise as serpents and innocent as doves, so we can continue to honor authorities and lawfully ignore the marriage license.*

Steps to Lawful Name Change

Again, you can always attempt Trish's method and simply apply for a name change, on the social security application, assuming the husband's last name.

If that is not the route you want to go, here are some ideas to help you in the process:

1. Acquire Legal Proof of a Name Change through the Superior Court System

In not using a marriage license you will need another form of legal evidence regarding the name change. You will need to go to the court and apply for a legal name change. This process is fairly easy once you know what you are doing. There will be an application and a fee.

A great website to determine your state's name change process is listed: www.uslegalforms.com/changeofname

The process and fee associated for each state is always a little different, state to state. Do your homework and follow the rules accordingly.

In the state of Kansas some of the restrictions listed from the website above are as follows:

"You may *not* obtain a name change in the state of Kansas for the purposes of avoiding debts, avoiding legal process, or to mislead or defraud any person. The district county court judge also reserves the right to deny your petition for name change, after reviewing the testimony, examining the evidence and reviewing the record."

Chances are, you have not or are not, doing anything of the sort listed above.

2. Social Security Number

Most people have a social security number.

If you are one of these people then you will need to visit the social security department and fill out some paper work to receive a new name, on your social security card. In the footer, is the link to the Social Security website for the form needed to change your name[31].

As you will read on the application for SS-5, simply put your new name in, put your previous name, your number and then fill out the rest.

[31] http://www.socialsecurity.gov/forms/ss-5.pdf

Mail the application in and wait to hear from them regarding your updated social security card.

3. Government ID

Next, you need to change your government records. The driver's license, if you have one, or your state identification is a great next move in the process of switching your name. Your passport is also another document you will want to update. The ideal way to change your name is to order your most important identification records to least important. After you do that, everything will fall into place.

4. Financial Accounts

Once you have updated your government records, social security card, state driver's license, passport, etc., then it should be straight forward changing all other documents. Your banking, stock and insurance accounts will be the next most important things to change.

5. Bills and Employment

Updating your bills and other company accounts is the next move in this process of changing your name. Here is a list of places you all want to update your files:

- Business
- Employer
- Electric and Utility Companies
- Credit Card Company
- Post Office
- Landlord or Mortgage Company
- Insurance Companies (auto, home, life)
- Doctors' Office
- Voter Registration Office
- Legal Documents
- Gym and Social Club Memberships
- Schools and Alumni Associations
- Email
- Social Websites, Facebook, Linkedin, Twitter, etc.

Keep in mind, this list is just an example of places you may need to go. It will become more clear, as you start to move forward, where you all need to make the appropriate changes.

COMMENTS FROM PASTOR MATT

In my research, I came across a Pastor's writings on the topic of marriage license, which is widely published across the internet, on multiple websites. I spoke with Pastor Matt, who over the years, has performed approximately 50 or so marriages, without a marriage license. I asked Pastor Matt, "Have there been any divorces and if so how many?" He indicated that there have been five divorces that he knows of as of the summer of 2011. He went on to say that of the five marriages, that ended in divorce, three of them went to court. Of the three that went to court, in each situation the court ruled the relationship a legal marriage.

I asked, "What caused the marriages to end in divorce, adultery?" He commented, "Usually one of the individuals wanted to rebel against God. None of the marriages ended because a spouse was unfaithful or committed adultery."

Notice only 10% of the marriages ended in divorce. Now I realize that the ideal is 0%. However, in today's world a 10% divorce rate is a far superior percentage, than the current norm under state marriage license contract. What is also encouraging, these couples in common law marriages were able to dissolve their marriage without battling it out with divorce lawyers or laboring the court system. That is infinitely more worthwhile in it of itself than what is offered via the marriage license terms and conditions.

Concluding Comments

In researching the topic of state marriage licenses, it became increasingly clear, the importance of not signing a marriage license. For those who choose to sign the marriage license they are:

1. Calling what God created a criminal activity – the marriage of a man and woman.

2. Yoking themselves to a three-party relationship with the state and their spouse.

3. Admitting they are not competent to handle their own relationship and family.

4. Making the state parent over their children.

5. There is no additional security in a marriage license vs. common law marriage.

For those looking for other options found in common law marriage, be assured:

1. Common law marriage is legal in all 50 states.

2. Common law keeps an unholy government out of the intimate details of your marriage relationship.

3. Marriage between a man and woman has always been legal in the eyes of God and mankind.

4. Couples are able to receive the same "benefits" as those with marriage licenses – such as filing taxes, buying homes or acquiring health insurance.

Followers of Jesus are being confronted with the questions, "How important is marriage and is marriage worth fighting for as God designed it? Will we keep our marriages together for the sake of our spouses, families and society? Will we keep our vows, as to the LORD?"

The body of Christ is the standard bearer for society. Marriage is not just for you, not just for you and your spouse, not just for you and your family, but for the LORD and all of society. There is strength added to society when a man and woman stay together in a committed relationship.

Will you raise the standard of holy matrimony to what it

was always intended to demonstrate? Holy matrimony is the most significant relationship anyone could enter into, reflecting the very image and nature of God. Take us back to the reverence of what this covenant was always designed to represent – a picture of oneness in God.

The Bible communicates clearly, this relationship is not easy and there will be troubles. For those of you who say, "Yes!" to this relationship, can you think of a better cause to fight for?

Father in Heaven, would You strengthen Your people? Let us be a people of perseverance, commitment, integrity and character. Let us be a people committed to You and Your Word. Let us seek first the kingdom of God and Your righteousness. Expose all deception-taking place within our lives. Let us be a people that take responsibility for our decisions. Holy Spirit, help us. Holy Spirit help marriages. Help marriages become what they can only be with Your presence. Let us be a people of purity. Purify Your Bride, LORD Jesus. The Spirit and the Bride say, "Come LORD Jesus come!" I ask in Your name, Jesus. Amen.

Recommended Reading and Resources

The Holy Bible, NKJV, Thomas Nelson Publishing

Longing For Eden, Mike and Anne Rizzo - marriagelongingforeden.com

The 5 Love Languages, Gary D. Chapman

Supernatural Marriage, Dan Wilson - supernaturalmarriage.org

Sacred Marriage, Gary Thomas

Love and Respect, Dr. Emmerson Eggerichs

Boundaries, Dr. Henry Cloud & Dr. John Townsend

Man of Steel and Velvet, Dr. Aubrey Andelin

Biblical Foundations of Freedom, Art Mathias

Freedom Immersion and Marriage Immersion, by Freedom City Church in Tacoma Washington - citycentral.org

Nothing Hidden Ministries, P.O.Box 992383, Redding, CA 96099 nothinghidden.com

The Cleansing Seminar, Dr. Timothy Davis - Cleansing the Church Ministries: PO Box 8326, Mission Hills, CA 91346 USA 818.833.7999

Reference

New King James Version, © 1982 by Thomas Nelson, Inc. All rights reserved. Used by permission.

THE HOLY BIBLE, NEW INTERNATIONAL VERSION®, NIV®
Copyright © 1973, 1978, 1984, 2011 by Biblica, Inc.®
Used by Permission of Biblica, Inc.® All rights reserved worldwide.

The Interlinear Bible, 4 volumes © 1976, 1977, 1978, 1979, 1980, 1981, 1984, 2nd Edition © 1985 by Jay P. Green, Sr. Hendrickson Publishers, Peabody, Massachusetts. Used by permission. All rights reserved.

By permission. From Merriam-Webster's Collegiate® Dictionary, 11th Edition ©2015 by Merriam-Webster, Inc. (www.Merriam-Webster.com).

By Permission Black's Law Dictionary, 10th ed. 2014

Chapter 1 - Origin and History of Marriage License

See Matthew 23:9
See John 3:3
See John 3:16
See Acts 8:37

The Marriage License by Dr. Benjamin E. Townsend

American Uniform Marriage and Marriage License Act

https://carm.org/list-of-roman-catholic-false-teachings
http://www.usccb.org/beliefs-and-teachings/what-we-believe/catechism/catechism-of-the-catholic-church/epub/index.cfm
http://www.vatican.va/archive/ENG0015/_INDEX.HTM
http://www.chick.com/information/religions/catholicism/
http://en.wikipedia.org/wiki/Marriage_license

"The Uniform Marriage and Divorce Act"
(UMDA)http://www.uniformlaws.org/shared/docs/Marriage%20and%20Divorce%20Act/UMDA%201973.pdf

Chapter 2 - Parens Patriae

Black's Law - Parens Patriae

Reference: TheFreeDictionary © 2015 by Farlex, Inc.
http://legal-dictionary.thefreedictionary.com/Parens+Patriae
http://www.breakingchristiannews.com/articles/display_art.html?ID=15067
http://medicalkidnap.com/2014/12/03/local-king-5-news-reports-on-rengo-family-children-being-medically-kidnapped/
http://www.hisholychurch.org/declarations/marriage/index.php/

Chapter 3 - Is the Government Holy

See Exodus 19:6 NKJV
See 1 Peter 1:15-16 NKJV
See 1 Peter 2:9 NKJV
See Ephesians 6:12 NKJV
See John 17:11-19 NKJV
See Psalm 37
See Psalm 139
See Jeremiah 29:11
See Deuteronomy 7:1-16

Conception of a Child, All Heaven Celebrates the Moment; T. Leverett - March 22, 2010

96 U.S. 76 - 24 L.Ed. 826 MEISTER v. MOORE October Term, 1877

Chapter 4 - Permission from the State

See Proverbs 3:5-7; 3:8-10
See John 10:10 NKJV
See 1Peter 5:8 NKJV
See Hosea 4:1-10 NKJV
See Habakkuk 2:2 NKJV

http://quotes.liberty-tree.ca/quote_blog/Peter.Hoagland.Quote.0FD8
http://www.wnd.com/2011/11/372409/#WovBFEAVQKBpU8SJ.99
http://www.ohiobar.org/Pages/LawFactsPamphletsDetail.aspx?itemID=35

96 U.S. 76 - 24 L.Ed. 826 MEISTER v. MOORE October Term, 1877

http://caselaw.findlaw.com/al-court-of-civil-appeals/1325717.html

Linneman v. Linneman, 1 Ill.App.2d 48, 50, 116 N.E.2d 182, 183 (1953),

Van Koten v. Van Koten, 323 Ill. 323, 326, 154 N.E. 146 (1926). □

Linneman, 1 Ill.App.2d at 50, 116 N.E.2d at 183. □

http://caselaw.findlaw.com/il-court-of-appeals/1486817.html#sthash.4KofxrrT.dpuf
https://amiracle42sisters.wordpress.com/2015/01/21/please-join-the-truth-train/

Chapter 5 - Adhesion Contract

Black's Law Dictionary, 10th ed. 2014

http://digitalcommons.law.ggu.edu/cgi/viewcontent.cgi?article=1877&context=ggulrev

Chapter 6 - The Fraud Matter

See Matthew 19:8 NKJV

96 U.S. 76 - 24 L.Ed. 826 MEISTER v. MOORE October Term, 1877

http://www.nationmaster.com/graph/peo_div_rat-people-divorce-rate
https://en.wikipedia.org/wiki/Religion_in_the_United_states
http://www.cookcountyclerk.com/vitalrecords/marriagelicenses/Pages/default.aspx
http://www.cookcountyclerk.com/vitalrecords/marriagelicenses/Pages/default.aspx
http://www.merriam-webster.com/dictionary/must
www.1215.org/lawnotes/misc/marriage/meister_v_moore_96_us_76.pdf
http://www.merriam-webster.com/dictionary/fraud

Chapter 7 - Laws of the Land

(MEYER v. STATE OF NEBRASKA, 262 U.S. 390 (1923)

See 1 Peter 5:8 NKJV
Uniform Marriage and Marriage License Act
Declaration of Independence – In Congress, July 4, 1776

Chapter 8 - Types of Legal Marriage

Common Law Marriage And It's Development in the United states - by Otto Erwin Koegel

http://www.originalintent.org/edu/marriage.php
Supreme Court case of Meister Vs. Moore in 1877
Black's Law Dictionary, 10th ed. 2014

Chapter 9 - How Can I Get Out?

American Uniform Marriage and Marriage License Act

See Romans 8:1 NKJV
See Acts 16:20-24 NKJV
See Ezekiel 22:23-26 NKJV
See James 4:4-10 NKJV

Chapter 10 - Divorce and Remarriage

See Psalm 15:1-5, 119 NKJV
See Matthew 5:29, 33-37 NIV
See Exodus 20:4-6,14 NKJV
See Leviticus 20:10 NKJV
See Deuteronomy 5:18 NKJV
See Proverbs 6:32 NKJV
See Jeremiah 3; 23:14-15 NKJV
See Ezekiel 23:37 NKJV
See Hosea 4
See Matthew 5:27-30; 10:28; *5:31-32; 19:3-10; 5:27-37* NKJV
See Revelation 2:20-23 NKJV
See Galatians 5:16
See James 4:4-6 NKJV
See John 8:3-11 NKJV

Meister vs. Moore in 1877

Chapter 11 - The Homosexual License

See Leviticus 20:13 NKJV
See Romans 1:24-32*, 10:9-11, 13* NKJV
See 2 Corinthians 6:14 NKJV
See 1Thessalonians 5:5 NKJV
See 1Corinthians 6:9-11 NKJV
See John 3:16, *3:3-5* NKJV
See Matthew 11:28-30 NKJV

http://www.care2.com/causes/what-states-allow-gay-marriage.html
http://gaymarriage.procon.org/view.resource.php?resourceID=004857
http://www.cnn.com/2013/05/28/us/same-sex-marriage-fast-facts

Chapter 12 - Changing Your Name is Easy

www.iowacourts.gov
http://www.change.name
http://www.uslegalforms.com/changeofname/
http://www.socialsecurity.gov/ssnumber/ss5.htm - Call - 1-800-772-1213
http://www.azleg.gov/ArizonaRevisedStatutes.asp?Title=1
https://www.legis.iowa.gov/DOCS/Central/Guides/marriage.pdf
https://www.ksbar.org/?marriage_divorce

Disclaimer:
This information is provided and sold with the knowledge that the publisher and author do not offer any legal or other professional advice. In the case of a need for any such expertise consult with an appropriate legal professional. This book does not contain all information available on the written subject matter. This book has not been created to be specific to any individual's or organizations' situation or needs. Every effort has been made to make this book as accurate as possible. However, there may be typographical, grammatical and or content errors. Therefore, this book should serve only as a general guide and not as the ultimate source of subject information. This book contains information that might be dated and is intended only to educate and entertain. The author and publisher shall have no liability or responsibility to any person or entity regarding any loss or damage incurred, or alleged to have incurred, directly or indirectly, by the information contained in this book. The author does not assume and hereby disclaims any liability to any party for any loss, damage, or disruption caused by errors or omissions, whether such errors or omissions result from accident, negligence, or any other cause. You hereby agree to be bound by this disclaimer or you may return this book in new condition.

ABOUT THE AUTHOR

Joshua Paul grew up in a Christian home where the Bible was read and their family prayed in Jesus' name. Graduating from a top 10 business school, he launched out into the world of entrepreneurialism by continuing with his online ecommerce business, which he started at the age of 20. Joshua also has years of experience working in the entertainment industry as a model and actor. Using God's gifts and talents, his goal was to reach those who would possibly never set foot in a church building. Eventually, Joshua began working with Christian non-profit ministries on a full-time basis where the Lord further developed, refined and cultivated his relationship with Jesus. Bouncing between the ministry and marketplace, Joshua now desires to use his gifts and talents to develop as a philanthropist, media entrepreneur and minister of the Word.

If you have appreciated and become informed by this book, look for Joshua Paul's next book "The Biblical Marriage: For God or Government?" to release shortly. This book will include this content, in addition he will discuss the origin of marriage, purpose of marriage, the courting process and his personal story of an engagement that ended over the marriage license discussion. Also included will be sample marriage certificates and contracts, not state related.

www.ingramcontent.com/pod-product-compliance
Lightning Source LLC
Chambersburg PA
CBHW070035100426
42740CB00013B/2699

* 9 7 8 0 6 9 2 4 3 9 3 7 1 *